An Armchair Fan's
Guide to the

QATAR
WORLD CUP

An Armchair Fan's
Guide to the

QATAR
WORLD CUP

The Story of How Football
Came to the Desert

Jon Berry

First published by Pitch Publishing, 2022

Pitch Publishing
A2 Yeoman Gate
Yeoman Way
Worthing
Sussex
BN13 3QZ
www.pitchpublishing.co.uk
info@pitchpublishing.co.uk

A CIP catalogue record is available for this book
from the British Library.

ISBN 978 1 80150 372 3

Typesetting and origination by Pitch Publishing
Printed and bound in Great Britain by TJ Books, Padstow

Contents

For all the builders forced to live in a bunk-bedded shack so that the stadia can glitter under an illuminated desert. For all their mates who didn't make it.

For the army of those on two dollars a day in Qatar and elswhere.

For every woman and every member of the LGBQT+ community in Qatar who might enjoy a few weeks free from anxiety and scrutiny … before the world moves on to the next circus.

For every kid who falls in love with the beautiful game: don't let them take it off you and then sell it back to you.

February 2022: final proof that sport couldn't be separated from politics

THIS BOOK was never going to be a glossy guide to the awe and wonder of the World Cup. The intention was always to put football, with its strange ways, daft quirks and its capacity to thrill beyond words, at the centre of everything. But it was never going to shy away from the grimy world of backroom dealing, hard economics and sly corruption that have been companions to everything that happens to the beautiful game at the highest level. It was always going to be a book that refused to subscribe to the notion that sport and politics don't mix.

The choice of Qatar as the venue for the competition made it inevitable, even for the most insular football fan, that issues such as labour abuses and civil liberties couldn't be separated in any preview of the World Cup in the desert. It would be absurd not to deal with them.

But this is still a football book. At those times during the writing when I thought the subject matter was getting lost in the political weeds, some pure footballing content was quickly hauled in to bring writer and reader back to the main matter in hand.

Most of the book had been written as we approached the end of February 2022. With final qualifying games around the world scheduled to be complete by the end of March, it was just going to be a matter of some final adjustments to comments about who would be present when the competition started in November.

And then, on the morning of 24 February, Russian troops invaded Ukraine. If scribbling about football had seemed frivolous beforehand, it now seemed positively imbecilic.

The football world reacted quickly. In doing so, it reflected the shock and outrage at Putin's actions, even before his troops began their devastating bombardments and sieges while Europe prepared for another refugee crisis. UEFA moved the Champions League final from St Petersburg; Manchester United severed its ties with Aeroflot; those teams due to play Russia in World Cup qualifiers categorically refused to do so; Dynamo Moscow's Fedor Smolov, with 45 caps and 16 goals for Russia, immediately condemned the invasion. In the coming weeks, as the UK government directed its theatre of condemnation of those rich Russians whose largesse they had once been happy to enjoy, Roman Abramovich was forced to relinquish his control of Chelsea. An early contender for the club's ownership was the Saudi Media Group, headed by 'Chelsea fan' Mohamed Alkhereiji, so football was clearly learning lessons about the probity of those allowed to oversee the game.

Football, like everyone in both politics and the wider sporting world, had been asleep at the wheel as far as Russia was concerned. Sure, Putin had already made incursions into bordering independent states. Yes, he was making belligerent noises as troops amassed on borders. But this was nothing more than the usual posturing from another of the globe's gang of hard-eyed, self-regarding – but dangerous – blowhards. Wasn't it? It had only been a few short years since the footballing world had turned the blindest of eyes and legitimised his regime by allowing its prime contest to be played out in his home territory. FIFA president, Gianni Infantino, who will feature later, was literally prepared to cuddle up to Putin (see photos) and whisper in his ear that 'The world has created bonds of friendship with Russia that will last forever.'

There is some dispute as to who first coined the term 'sportswashing' but if there was ever uncertainty as to its meaning, too much has happened since the 2018 World Cup to leave any doubt as to its existence. Rockets were launched at Kyiv just days after China had staged its low-key winter Olympics, having escaped any meaningful scrutiny or protest over its human rights record. The organisers in Qatar may have felt a tremor of misgiving that the real world could spoil their party, but only needed to look west to their neighbours in Saudi Arabia and south to Yemen. As Europe shuddered at Putin's actions, Yemenis on the end of British armaments still failed to feature on any news bulletin. The great and the good in Doha could relax. War and devastation weren't going to get in the way of football.

On Sunday 13 March, Chelsea played Newcastle at Stamford Bridge. A section of the Chelsea fans thought it appropriate to chant their loyalty to Abramovich while, among the Newcastle supporters, some waved Saudi flags and sang 'we're richer than you'. To give that small minority the benefit of the doubt, news of the 81 executions by the Saudi government on 12 March may not yet have reached them. What's more, the loyalists and the flag-wavers may well have been a minority. Nevertheless, it was an uncomfortable episode redolent of sport's enduring belief that it can slide through life in its isolated bubble.

So, to use the time-honoured disclaimer, all footballing facts are correct at the time of going to press. As for the future of civilised society, we're all holding our breath.

April 2022

Chapter 1

Qatar. Some useful stuff to know, starting with where it is

(Look closely, it's very small)

HOSNI MUBARAK was President of Egypt for 30 years until 2011. He had a very low opinion of Qatar. He once told its ruler that he wasn't worth any of his precious time. 'Why should I bother talking with someone whose country has the population of a small hotel?' he sneered. In 1999, he visited the bedraggled, dusty headquarters of rookie broadcasters Al Jazeera in the capital, Doha. 'This matchbox!' he exclaimed. 'All this noise coming out of this matchbox?'

Mubarak hadn't exactly read the runes on Qatar. In his head it was probably still an insignificant appendage on the Arabian Gulf, with a backward economy dependent on pearl-fishing and the export of dates. By the time he was scuttling away from his presidential palace, displaced by the uprisings of the Arab Spring in 2011, Qatar was well on the way to becoming a major player on the global stage – and one of the main agents trumpeting this prominence was Al Jazeera. At the start of 2022, the station claimed to have over 40 million regular viewers in the Arab world and to have a reach into 270 million households in 140 countries.

The significant soft power exercised by Al Jazeera is backed up by enormous wealth. Qatar became a British protectorate in 1916 during the First World War, gaining independence in 1971 when it had ceased, in the eyes of its protector, to be of any strategic value. At around the same time, the huge discoveries of oil and offshore gas deposits were being harnessed to transform the nation's economic power. It now enjoys the fourth-highest Gross Domestic Product (GDP) per capita in the world. This calculation is slightly misleading on account of one of Qatar's significant peculiarities: at least 85 per cent of its overall population of 2.8 million consists of migrant workers and ex-pats. It's fair to say that this wealth is not spread around in an equitable fashion.

The country is an absolute monarchy, currently under the leadership of Sheikh Tamim bin Hamad Al-Thani, who has been in power since 2013. Islam is the official religion and it is a deeply conservative society, governed by a mixture of civil and Sharia law. It does, however, seem to avoid the worst excesses of hanging, flogging and other mediaeval practices still to be found in the region, favouring instead financial penalty for punishment. It is keen to demonstrate to the rest of the world that it is ridding itself of other vestiges of backward practices, although, as we'll see, it has some way to go.

It is not a country that is over-worried about what the neighbours think, other than to get one over on them. Its support for Iran and some Islamic groups has made for frosty relationships with Saudi Arabia, Bahrain, Egypt and the United Arab Emirates. In a strange but alarming take on political choreography, it accommodates the air base of Al Udeid, a logistics and basing hub for US operations in Afghanistan, while simultaneously serving as the location for peace talks with the Taliban. Reports abound of representatives of these religious zealots happily partaking of the finer things in life in Doha's gleaming metropolis, both within and beyond local law.

It's very hot. Temperatures in the high summer months, which is when the World Cup was originally supposed to be contested, are consistently above 40°C from dawn to sunset. In November, when the competition starts, the average is 30°C, dropping to 25°C when most games will be played in December. There is a national football league – the Qatar Stars League – consisting of two divisions with promotion and relegation. Matches are played between September and April (yes, because it's too hot to play in summer) and the league's most famous player is Akram Afif, who plays for Al Sadd, the winner of 15 of the league's 49 seasons.

As for all the other interesting stuff you need to know about this tiny country, like corruption, workers' rights, player protest, who might win and, crucially, the price and availability of beer, all will be fully revealed in the pages that follow.

Chapter 2

Global contests in the sand dunes. How the desert put itself on the sporting map

FOOTBALL, CRICKET, golf and, at a pinch, rugby. Tennis, snooker and darts. Horseracing, and even, just about, show jumping. Boxing, yes, definitely boxing. Most of the stuff you come across at the Olympics, get hooked on and immediately feel emboldened to make expert judgements about. These are all sports I consider to be in my orbit, any of which I'd occasionally stop to watch when idly channel-surfing. But there is one pursuit that fails to hold my attention for even the most fleeting nanosecond. Formula One motor racing.

There is no doubting the physicality, intense levels of concentration and, above all, iron-nerved bravery required to participate. In terms of rampant commercialism, dubious ethical practices and the repellent nature of its stars and backers, it's no worse than any other sport. It has millions of aficionados around the world, most of whom probably regard, for example, cricket as an arcane pastime and its patrons as quaintly misguided and intellectually challenged. The fortunate audiences who pay astronomical entrance fees to watch races live probably can't fathom why committed enthusiasts of other sports shell out similar amounts to watch something they regard as boring, repetitive and entirely lacking in meaningful action.

So it was, that on a dullish weekend in November 2021, shortly after I embarked on planning this book, I forced myself to take an interest in the Qatar Grand Prix. A few days earlier, England's footballers had cemented their place in the World Cup final stages with a ruthless but farcical 10-0 win against San Marino, with Scotland and Wales giving themselves a fighting chance of joining them. The finals in Qatar, which had previously seemed somewhat notional, began to take on a more concrete feel. A few days earlier, the governing bodies of England's professional leagues had announced earlier starts than usual to the 2022/23 season. There were telling gaps in fixture lists in November and December. That really did begin to make it real. For the first time as a normal-ish football supporter – and I don't think I'm alone here – I began to take a more acute interest in the World Cup in Qatar.

Like many people, I'd hazily followed stories about human rights abuses and dubious governmental practices. I'd been lucky enough to have been on a couple of brief work trips to Dubai (didn't like it) and had some microscopically faint knowledge of the region. Given that I'm a news hound, I reckoned I had a decent grasp of some of the geopolitics of the Middle East, but, really and truly, if pressed on the subject, my knowledge about Qatar was alarmingly faint. What's more, I was pretty certain that I wasn't on my own in this regard and so I set out to do something about it as the World Cup approached.

Was there anything to learn on that lost afternoon of the Qatar Grand Prix? Even as a motor-racing refuser, I was aware that a good deal of crucial action had taken place before the race began. Qualifying rounds had allocated drivers differing levels of advantage on the starting grid. This whole process had generated the imposition of penalties, all of which, in regulation sporting behaviour, had been hotly disputed by the aggrieved parties. Then David Beckham turned up – because it seems kind of obligatory to wheel him out on such occasions – resplendent and cool in a beautiful blue suit under the desert sun, posing with the World Cup trophy. He had a little hug with Qatari businessman, former minister without portfolio and chairman of Paris Saint-Germain, Nasser Al-Khelaifi (we'll hear a lot more about him later) and glad-handed a load of other blokes, some of whom had been the subject of the Sky commentator's homework and some others who had not. It's fair to say I wasn't hooked.

In another pre-race episode, Lewis Hamilton, who had already alienated a significant part of the petrol-head world by proudly sporting a Black Lives Matter t-shirt, donned a rainbow-coloured helmet. Just in case there was any chance of anyone underplaying the importance of his action, he posted pictures of him wearing it with the message 'we stand together' to his ten million followers on Twitter and Instagram. 'An incredible act of allyship,' commented racing driver Richard Morris, founder of Pride in Racing, and one that 'fills me with hope'. No recorded comment seemed available from anyone else and certainly no official rebuke from any source close to the racing authorities. The Qatari government, which, like so many in the region, presides over highly discriminatory laws against women and LGBTQ+ people, remained equally shtum.

The race began as dusk lowered over a grey November afternoon in the UK, but with the sun having fully settled in the Gulf. The venue, Lusail, some 20km north of the capital, Doha, is set around a planned city and will be home to one of the major World Cup venues. Light flooded the racetrack on this reclaimed land. Masses of light. 'The equivalent of 3,600 light bulbs,' gushed the race commentator – and, surely, I can't have been the only dad listening thinking, 'Well, don't bloody well forget to turn them off when you're finished then.' Such prosaic matters weren't really on the minds of the faithful, either in studios or the arena in the desert.

In an age where apprehension about energy consumption has ceased to be a niche concern, the coverage of this miracle of illumination on the website of Red Bull, a major sponsor of the sport, was a bit of an eyebrow-raiser. The thousands of bulbs were powered by 44 13-megawatt generators (no, me neither) and supported by 500km of wiring. Enough, apparently, to provide power for 3,000 homes. Red Bull declines to tell us for how long, but one assumes until Armageddon or something equally unpropitious. To help us contextualise this marvel, we're informed that this is enough to light a residential street stretching from Doha to Moscow – some, 3,500km. The patrons of the sport revel unapologetically in such extravagance, all of which will be replicated in a myriad of ways when football comes to town.

I'll come clean. I didn't pay that much attention as the cars buzzed round the track like angry wasps. Almost inevitably to my untutored eye, Lewis Hamilton – this time helmeted in the livery of more commercial enterprises – crossed the line first, thus keeping the drivers' championship alive by closing the gap on his rival, Max Verstappen. The Grand Prix circus prepared to pack up and set off for the two final races in the tournament: contests in Saudi Arabi and Abu Dhabi would complete the 'desert trilogy'. Oddly – and this, of course, is often the way with newly piqued interests – I found myself being faintly invested in what might happen next.

The plain fact remained, however, that if I was looking for mainstream media coverage to make any attempt to cross the line between sport, politics and social issues, my brush with Formula One had revealed nothing. This tiny knot of land, slightly smaller than Yorkshire, tacked on to the Arabian Peninsula, had just staged its first major global sporting event and it was going on to greater things. Its big brother next door in Saudi Arabia had just weighed in with the purchase of Newcastle United. It had already usurped world boxing's favoured venues to host Anthony Joshua's victory against Andy Ruiz Jnr in December 2019 – a bout reported to have enriched Joshua by some £20m. It had still not abandoned hope of staging an all-British fight between Joshua and Tyson Fury. But Qatar had made an even bigger breakthrough. The world's gaze would soon be fully upon it and it was going to work hard to don its most respectable face.

As it began to do so, followers of high-level competition were becoming ever more familiar with the concept of sportswashing – the staging of prestigious events as a way of demonstrating to the wider world that hosts of competitions, or the owners of clubs, were legitimate, honest and part of a progressive, modern world. This book poses some awkward questions about whether some of these claims are valid and, on occasion, provides some answers. What it doesn't do is pretend to be a forensic and detailed analysis of negotiations, bribery and malpractice that have been an unwelcome part of staging World Cups, particularly in the current era. A host of dedicated investigative journalists and authors have already done a much more thorough job than I could've done. Wherever I have drawn on their work, I have acknowledged it, and I do so with gratitude.

This is a book for football fans who want to see the landscape against which the World Cup in the desert will play out. It'll take you from the Maracana to Swindon's County Ground via Wembley and North Korea before ending up in the Khalifah in Doha. There are plenty of football stories, scurrilous (but accurate) comment about some of the villains leeching off the game and, because it's football, it's littered with my own juvenile, irrational prejudices – some of which I hope you'll share.

This isn't intended as an academic book and neither is it quite *The Qatar World Cup for Dummies*. It's an attempt to place the entire event in a wider political, societal and, most importantly, footballing context, without getting dragged too far into the vortex that each and every aspect of it presents. I've identified the leads and sources for my information and an inquisitive reader can find the greater depth available by following any of these. It also goes without saying that I started the story of the book with absolutely no idea about how it would end: 'work in progress' doesn't even begin to cover it.

So, as promised, into the launderette of sport.

* * *

Verstappen got a last-minute Grand Prix winner, just in case you a) care and b) didn't know already.

Chapter 3

Nazi propaganda, post-war defiance, national pride and the (disputed) nutritional value of whale meat. Some history about what's to be gained when hosting the party

ON THE evening of Friday, 27 July 2012, I made a point of going out for a drink. There was no crisis in my life or any point of tension that made me determined to leave the house. The reason was that I really, really didn't want to watch the telly. It turned out to be a big mistake.

The event that I had been so desperate to avoid was the opening of the Olympic Games in London. It wasn't just the tedium of the athletes' parade that held no attraction. I just knew – and before history gets indelibly rewritten, I wasn't on my own here – that the ceremony itself was likely to be cringe-worthy on a number of levels: stuffy, sentimental, ploddingly patriotic, backward-looking and static. Wrong on all counts.

Danny Boyle's vibrant, witty and inclusive spectacle was a joy – and one that has endured, even if it already provokes a rather wistful nostalgia for a bygone era. It set the tone for the weeks that followed, which were best summed up by the frequently voiced observation that it was like living in a foreign country – a place where the trains really did run on time and people greeted you with a smile. What's more, the nation's athletes performed as well as they had ever done. Even better, we had been told, the Games would leave a legacy for generations to come, revitalising and renovating a dowdy and depressed part of East London.

Opinion is divided about the existence of any such legacy, beneficial or not. The website of the International Olympic Committee posts a gleaming five-minute video that talks of the 110,000 jobs that have been brought to the area, along with the million people who have visited the site since 2012. It points to the number of volunteers who have continued to offer their services elsewhere in other communities. Among the footage of local kids playing on all-weather surfaces and swimmers ploughing along in the same pool where champions still train, green spaces abound, educational establishments flourish and local young people speak glowingly of apprenticeship opportunities.

It may just be that the Olympic Committee's publicity machine is hugging too much credit to itself. The Stratford City Project was launched in the late 1990s, some time before London's successful bid for the Games in 2005. The impetus was the construction of the new high-speed rail link out of St Pancras and a recognition of the need to address the crumbling infrastructure and wider needs of that part of London. The leader of the committee charged with developing the Olympic Park, Jason Prior, was on record at the time as stating that most of the development would have taken place irrespective of hosting the Games.

The spruce boulevards and outdoor cafes of the promotional video are mostly located in pseudo-public spaces – large squares, parks and thoroughfares that might appear to be public but are, in fact, owned and controlled by developers and corporations. Of the 2,800 houses built in the area since the Games, half are earmarked as affordable dwellings. This widely derided measure, which sets rents at 80 per cent of the market value, has become an increasingly discredited and ridiculous notion in London and the South East. The half that are on the open market operate under the auspices of Get Living London, who represent the interests of the owners, Qatari Diar.

On balance, it might be reasonable to suggest that, although there may be differing perspectives on the legacy of London's Games, to borrow from the Hippocratic Oath, they did no harm. They certainly avoided the logistical calamities of Atlanta or the generation of waste ground in Athens, which prompted Belgian photographer Brecht De Vleeschauwer, surveying the ruinous landscape, to observe that, 'Olympic investments are always presented as beneficial for all, but if we see this kind of scene we can think twice.' London might not have generated the questionable claims of the Spanish Trails website that the Barcelona games were instrumental in transforming 'what was formerly a struggling city' into one that 'has now gained international acclaim for its beauty, culture, and unique amenities'. It has probably turned out closer to the cheery assessment of Australia's ABC news network about Sydney's Games that 'what we really got for $6.5bn was a big party and the glowing memories we are now sharing'.

The summer Olympics and the football World Cup are the two premium global SMEs – Sports Mega-Events. The decision about who hosts them has now become an overblown soap opera. It's a show reliant, for audience appeal, on shenanigans that set the gold standard for complexity, opacity; all of which is irretrievably mired in corruption, lobbying and malpractice. Which begs a central question: what are the perceived advantages that prompt nations to participate in the circus of bidding for these two major SMEs?

A convenient, albeit contested, place to define the start of the 'modern era' in sport is the Second World War. The SMEs either side of this shattering event provide useful illustrations as to why a nation should present itself as a prospective host. In 1936 the Summer Olympics were held in Berlin when Hitler's National Socialists were bedding in as Germany's government. The Fuhrer was determined to use the Games as a vehicle to display his nation's phoenix-like revival after its military defeat in 1918. This has been widely documented, with many significant events and episodes available on newsreel. A rare but inspiring moment of relief in this grim portrayal of dark times is provided by the Black athlete Jesse Owens, whose dominance on the track punctured Hitler's notion of Aryan supremacy, with the evidence of his grimacing discomfiture clearly captured on film. Nonetheless, the use of the Games to showcase the outward respectability of the Nazi regime was considered a clear success by the country's rulers. When England's footballers acceded to the request to give the Nazi salute prior to an international game in Berlin two years later, Hitler and his officials must have smiled at a job well done.

If Hitler was determined to use the event as a display to both Germans and a wider audience of his nation's potency, the first Olympics after the war told a different but equally illustrative story. The 1948 Games took place in London after a low-key bidding process involving the USA, Switzerland and the UK during 1939. No Rolexes had been popped into goody bags, no designer handbags placed discreetly on meeting-room seats and no late-night calls to hotel rooms had come from Lonely Luscious Lulu. Despite the ravages of war, still immediately apparent on the bombed-out streets of a capital still subject to food-rationing, the firm decision was taken that the show would most definitely go on. Hitler's extravagant triumphalism had given place to dogged, low-key determination.

Participating athletes were advised to bring as much food with them as possible as the only unrationed meat available in London was whale flesh. Unpalatable as it may have been, British 220-yard runner Sylvia Cheesman, in common, no doubt, with many of her contemporaries, could afford no concessions to a delicate palate: 'It was horrible, but I was so intent on getting my protein that I ate it.' Such nose-holding dedication did her no good. Despite reaching the semi-final, she failed to progress in an event in which the gold medal was won by the star of the Games, Fanny Blankers-Koen from the Netherlands. Britain's Audrey Williamson took the silver, but no record exists of her dietary preferences.

No new stadia or facilities were built – Wembley was the main arena for much of the action – and as well as food, competitors, housed in basic student halls-ofresidence, were told to bring their own towels. The BBC paid a princely £1,000 for the broadcasting rights and the opening ceremony was celebrated with the release of thousands of pigeons – which is kind of what I was expecting in July 2012. Yet for it all, these post-war Games, hidebound by genuine austerity and offering no frills or fanciness to either spectators or participants, did something that has not happened since – they turned a profit.

Writing in July 2021, prior to the post-Covid Tokyo Games, the economist Stefan Szymanski, professor of economics at the Cass Business School, noted that the 'IOC's model of the Olympics has become unsustainable' and goes on to observe that it 'is great for the athletes, the broadcasters, the sponsors and the sports administrators – but costly, unfair and unworkable for cities'. Price comparisons from different eras that attempt to bundle together differing goods, changing social attitudes and uneven economic progress are usually unhelpful, so maybe it's just best to go with the raw figures. A budget of £743,000 was set for the London event and, amazingly by modern standards, there was an underspend of just under £10,000. For some icing on the cake, receipts, mainly from ticket sales, generated nearly £762,000 and so a hefty of profit of £30,000 accrued. Unvarnished as they may have been, London's 1948 Olympics genuinely marked the end of era.

The Second World War marked a watershed in terms of Olympic hosting. The move had been made from the vainglorious use of the event by fascists and a dictator to defiant determination from democrats, albeit battered and skint ones. There is some correspondence when it came to the two football World Cups either side of the 1939–45 period, but if the 1948 Games seem a touch quaint to modern observers, the last football competition prior to the war transports us back to an entirely alien universe.

England didn't qualify for the 1938 World Cup in Paris. Not because they let in a last-minute equaliser in Latvia or got caught on the break by Slovenia at Wembley and failed to score despite battering them for 80 minutes, hitting both posts and the crossbar. They didn't appear because they didn't enter the competition. They hadn't done so in 1930 or in 1934 either. In a situation redolent of inter-war confidence, arrogance and haughty isolation, England had refused to become part of FIFA. Well, what would be the point in engaging in such nonsense? Nevertheless, they were offered an open invitation to the 1934 competition in Italy, the second such tournament, but still declined. The hosts won that competition and the following November accepted an invitation to play England at Highbury, Arsenal's home ground. The press dubbed the game 'the real World Cup final' and in a notoriously violent affair, England ran out 3-2 winners.

So, they really were world champions after all, then. So that was OK.

By the time of the tournament in 1938 in France, the world had taken a few turns for the worse – and England still weren't members of FIFA and, presumably because they were obviously world champions having beaten Italy at the Battle of Highbury, why would they need to be? There were already other notable absentees. Peeved by the decision to locate the competition in Europe, despite an understanding that South America would host the event, Uruguay and Argentina stayed at home. Spain was being riven by the Civil War that still echoes in *El Clasico* matches between Barcelona and Real Madrid and so were unable to field a team. And in middle-Europe, Austria had become the victim of the Anschluss, the annexation of their lands by Hitler's troops. Once again FIFA extended an invitation to England to fill one of these vacant spots – and once again the world champions declined.

In 14 days between 5 and 19 June, 13 teams played a straight knock-out competition for the non-English version of the World Cup, which was retained by Italy. Sweden, due to play Austria, were given a bye in the first round, which featured appearances from Cuba and the Dutch East Indies. The latter's journey from south-east Asia ended in a 6-0 thumping in the first round from Hungary, who went on to become beaten finalists. Had England been around to watch how the Mighty Magyars were developing their game, they may have avoided the two post-war poundings they received at their hands. As for Sweden, whether it was the extra preparation afforded them by not playing their first tie or the fact that Cuba had already played 90 minutes with extra time plus a replay in the seven days before they met, they brushed them aside 8-0 before losing to Hungary in the next round.

Eighteen games in 14 days, some played in front of four-figure crowds in locations resembling picturesque little grounds from the lower reaches of the English pyramid, fringed with trees and a decorous crowd just a few feet away from the touchline. Mainly men, they are trimly turned out in suits, ties and jaunty hats, although in more bohemian Marseilles, something of the rakish open-collar look can be detected. All of this is captured in Rene Lucot's glorious 30-minute film, which, although disputed as such, is regarded as the official FIFA record. Goalkeepers in polo-necks, flat caps and stripy socks handle the plunking caseball of a lost era without a glove in sight before booting it as far into the opposition half as possible. There are no numbers on players' shirts and so it is impossible to identify the Brazilian player sporting a pre-prototype Mohican and, along with the rest of his team-mates, skipping along in dainty shorts that are half the length of any donned by their opponents. Blazered referees saunter around close enough to the action and, in contrast to the frantic attention of modern physiotherapists and the application of controlled nutrition during games, in the lull between full-time and the extra half hour, players loll on the pitch in flat exhaustion, occasionally squeezing a sponge over their heads. At least none of them light up a ciggy.

A year after the 1938 final, the events that had prevented the participation of Austria and Spain had developed into the full force of world war. Two years later than the London Olympics, the first post-war FIFA World Cup took place in Brazil in the summer of 1950, fulfilling the pledge to alternate between Europe and South America. This time, having won the Home Nations Championship, which served as a qualifying competition, England deigned to participate. In an episode soaked in quirky irony given their volatile qualification record since, the Scottish Football Association, whose second place in this domestic contest merited a place in the finals, declined to attend for reasons that lie in the grave of its then chairman, George Graham. Goodness only knows what his namesake, who made such a mark on the game in years to come but never had the chance to play for his country on such a stage, would have made of it.

If the 1948 Olympics bore the hallmark of an event still anchored to the post-war world, its footballing counterpart displays many of the more commercially savvy traits that came to characterise its later manifestations. The format of four qualifying groups feeding one final group was specifically designed to generate more matches and, quite correctly as it turned out, more games featuring the hosts. This resulted in average crowds of over 61,000, which served to offset the expenditure incurred by teams negotiating fixtures spread over the 3,500km between Porto Alegre and Recife – a challenge replicated when Brazil hosted again in 2014.

The Brazilian authorities also enjoyed a stroke of luck. The four-team, six-game final group with simultaneous final matches threw up a clear decider, with Brazil and Uruguay going into the contest with points totals already unattainable by either Spain or Sweden. It meant that the game between Uruguay and Brazil on 16 July 1950 became a bona fide, winner-takes-all final watched by 199,954 people in the Maracana stadium. Almost all of them would have gone home miserable after the visitors came from behind to win 2-1. The defeat, dubbed the Maracanazo, prompted suicides (allegedly) and fighting in the streets. A red-faced Jules Rimet himself, the man after whom the trophy was named, had to abandon his prematurely penned speech, written in Portuguese in anticipation of a Brazilian victory.

And England? Well, the world champions started well enough with a 2-0 win against Chile, drawing just 170,000 fewer spectators than those who watched the final in the same location. Four days later, a crowd of 10,151 witnessed their utter humiliation when a Joe Gaetjens goal in the 38th minute in Belo Horizonte earned the United States a 1-0 victory. It is possible from the current period, when the leaders of the free world have made a decent fist of their place on the world soccah scene, to think that the extent of this surprise may seem overstated. It is not. There is a myth that in days when global communication clunked and limped along creaking newslines, English editors believed that 0-1 should really have read 10-1 and printed that result accordingly. A deflated England travelled back to Rio to try to save face, but lost 1-0 to Spain and went home.

Sixty years after the USA defeat, almost to the day, the fixture was repeated at the World Cup in South Africa. When the likeable Rob Green dived over Clint Dempsey's dribbly, scuffy effort to gift the USA an unlikely point, the ghost of Joe Gaetjens must have had a quiet chuckle.

Did anyone profit financially from either of football's pre- and post-war SMEs? There exists nothing like the open and public record-keeping of London's Olympics to provide such information. The principal global finance houses, most of whom have engaged in systematic forecasting and forensic analysis of World Cup finance since, hold no detailed records prior to the 1982 competition in Spain. There will certainly have been bar owners and hoteliers for whom such large events would have been welcome cash generators, but broadcasting rights would have been inconsequential. Lucot's film of the French tournament furnishes us with a group photo of the FIFA delegation in Paris. It is unsurprising in its depiction of contented white, male portliness and they, no doubt, enjoyed the benefit of their status in a range of ways. But from all the film and documentary evidence, two factors emerge.

First, nobody made a pot of money from advertising rights. Film of a few of the matches in France in 1938 give us a glimpse of a couple of billboards for Dubonnet – a sickly aperitif later imbued with faux sophistication in the UK with the catchy slogan in mock-French to 'do 'ave a Dubonnet'. We'll never know whether the vintners had to submit a closed bid for such a monopoly. Second, if London had managed to send a message of proud defiance to the rest of the world through its hosting of the Olympics, Brazil's World Cup was an event staged principally to impress a domestic audience. The country was acting as host a mere 56 years since the first game ever staged there. The Maracana was solid proof of its status as a country capable of producing a stadium to vie with any in the world – even if the final game was played with scaffolding still visible around many of the stands. Global telecommunication took hours, not nanoseconds and, besides, only 13 countries actually took part. Looking inward was the sensible thing to do: it was a Brazilian World Cup for Brazilians. It was left to football to have the last laugh when the final victory slipped away from the hosts.

Even though these four early prototypes of SMEs that bridged the Second World War belong to a distant, grainy world, each of them laid some stepping-stones to the future. Hitler's Berlin Games have become the byword for the use of sport as naked propaganda for both a domestic and international audience. London's Games did much the same, albeit in a more muted way and without the vile strutting and evil intent as the backdrop. Brazil, playing to its own audience, did at least have one of the world's most iconic stadia as its legacy. And France? Well, to cite Australia's ABC, although nothing like $6.5bn was shelled out, maybe they did just have a last-chance saloon, pre-war party and a few memories – and maybe, just maybe, that was the right way to go about it with the world on the brink of catastrophe. In the 80 years or so that followed, bidders limiting themselves to that cheery expectation might have saved plenty of people from defiling themselves by touching the pitch of bidding, backhanding and bribery that has so besmirched the award of the modern SME.

Which brings us to the $64bn question. How did the Qataris become serious contenders, why was their bid successful – and what do they think is in it for them?

Chapter 4

How football left home. In which the rest of the world loosens the hosting grip of Europe and South America

HE WAS there again, David Beckham. As elegant as ever, decked out in the regulation dark suit and burgundy tie of England's all-male presentation team at FIFA's palace in Zurich on 2 December 2010. Prince William and David Cameron had preceded him at the rostrum. His was the final attempt to woo the executive members to vote for the 2018 World Cup and persuade them to stage it at the home of the glimmering Premier League. As it turns out, this oddball collection of royal eminence, plump-faced Tory chumminess and football's fading demi-god had been sprats swimming with sharks. Outflanked and gobbled up by competitors, they found themselves squeezing out the sheepish, defeated grin of UK Eurovision competitors as they resumed their nul-points seats in the auditorium.

There they would have to sit, clenching all parts of their anatomies that can clench, as Sepp Blatter, enjoying the power moments for which his corruption-drenched office existed, opened the envelope to reveal Russia as the winners. Igor Shuvalov, the deputy prime minister, took to the stage flanked by his delegation, all of whom could have been auditioning for parts as KGB agents, other than the leopard-skin-clad beauty who would have been up for the part of the femme fatale. 'You will never regret this decision,' Igor promised, as Roman Abramovich nodded sagely behind him. And, as it turns out, he was just about right. As World Cups go, it managed to put on a pretty good show. From the spring of 2022, however, it all makes for some grim reflection.

As the triumphant Russians took their seats, the process for announcing the hosts of the 2022 tournament began. No reader in their right mind would want to look again at Blatter, fuddling and mumbling like a dishevelled uncle having his say at Christmas dinner and just about managing to extract the winning name from the envelope. Much more uplifting is to watch Alex Klim's brief film taken in the Souq in Doha as the moment is played on the big screen. Against the beguiling background of the black desert sky, silhouetted with the outlines of bridges and skyscrapers, the moment is greeted with wild enthusiasm by a flag-waving crowd, many of whom jump into their cars and begin a cacophonous parade around the adjoining streets. It may not have been the eco-friendliest of episodes, but it was one that spoke of spontaneous joy and pride. While that was also on show from the Qatari delegation in Zurich, it was in stark contrast to the sour, dulled faces of the others around them. Each, no doubt, clenching for all they were worth.

Before we delve into the filth and malpractice that is now synonymous with SMEs across so many sports, it's worth considering why the award to a nation in the Arabian Gulf caused such a spontaneously negative reaction from so many in Europe and the West. Without being too homespun about it, a good place to begin is with maps on the classroom wall.

Readers of a certain age will recall being told to look upon such maps with pride and rejoice in the amount of red – the colour assigned to the British Empire – that we could see. All such representations, including those printed long after the Britannia no longer ruled the waves, depict the world with Europe, and more particularly the United Kingdom, smack in the middle. The first time you ever encounter representations of the world when in different countries – China, Russia, the USA – there is a disorientating moment until it finally clicks that these nations see themselves as the centre of things. It is their country that is in the middle of the map. In footballing terms, too, it is a mindset that takes some shifting.

The previous chapter revealed two clear instances of how this had previously played out. The first of these was the long period of closed-shop World Cup hosting between Europe and South America, even though the latter was, itself, a relative new kid on the block. It might have been quaint to see others from exotic footballing outposts trying to elbow their way into the playing part of the competition, but the hosting power blocks were very clearly defined. Taking the tournament out of these agreed areas was simply never considered as a serious proposition.

The second issue related to England. As we saw, even though the pre-war World Cup was a slight, almost parochial affair in comparison to its modern counterpart, England's refusal to engage at any level reeks of the sense of entitlement and splendid isolationism that has so irritated its enemies and critics for decades. Despite the calamity at Belo Horizonte and indifferent performances at subsequent competitions, when England did win in 1966, there existed a widespread, largely unchallenged notion that, albeit somewhat tardily, the correct order of things had been restored. It's an idea still embodied in Baddiel and Skinner's chorus, churned out, usually with absolutely no sense of irony, for a few lager-fuelled days of summer at every tournament until the inevitable occurs.

When it comes to the homecoming of 1966, I speak of something I almost know. By that time, at 13 years of age, I was a regular at St Andrew's, an affliction that has clung like an itchy infection since. In one of those episodes from childhood that doggedly survive, I can vividly recall a conversation walking to school prior to the World Cup, debating whether we would sooner England triumph or the Blues win the FA Cup. Different days, of course, when the latter competition really did represent glamour and success. Any true-blooded club supporter does not need me to insult them by providing the unanimous outcome of this high-level symposium. But when we weren't discussing England's prospects, there was one team that we, and millions of others, took to our hearts. Exotic, unfamiliar and tiny North Korea.

Which was not what they wanted to be called. Representatives of the Democratic People's Republic of Korea had to negotiate with FIFA as well as the British Foreign Office before settling on this more convenient label. It was the latter institution that felt it prudent to recommend to the footballing authorities that 'the North Koreans will probably object very strongly if they are prevented from playing their national anthem and displaying their national flag, when the other 15 countries taking part in the finals are all permitted to do so'.

All of which provides something of a reminder. The 1966 competition may not have taken place in the immediate shadow of war in the same way that the 1948 Olympics did, but global conflict was still firmly lodged in the memory of plenty of people – although perhaps not so firmly in that of a blithely self-centred 13-year-old. Many of the besuited crowds who took the diminutive Koreans to their collective bosom in 1966 would have seen active service, some may even have been involved in the conflict between North and South Korea that ended after three years in 1953. They might have been rubbing their eyes at the sight of a team from that part of the world playing with the big boys.

There were no African nations represented. All eligible African countries boycotted the competition. Just to underline the point, not just one nation, but an entire continent refused to participate. As football historian Alan Tomlinson observed, 'Right from the very beginning, this was a story about cultural politics in the post-colonial period.' In other words, should anyone wish to study the roots of politics in sport, then a World Cup staged in the aftermath of a world war and the break-up of Empire is as good a place to start as any. And anyone labouring under the misapprehension that the fuddled, antiquarian approach of FIFA is anything new, could do worse than have a squint at the geopolitical background to the events of 1966.

FIFA had decided that the finals should be contested by ten teams from Europe, including the hosts. Four would come from South America, which included the holders, Brazil, one from central America and one from … wait for it … the whole of Africa, Asia and Oceania. African nations were already aggrieved by the fact that the previous winners of their qualifying competition, Morocco, had been forced into an unsuccessful play-off against Spain to get to Chile in 1962. The ire of the member nations of the Confederation of African Football, CAF, was then further enflamed when FIFA decided to admit South Africa to its ranks in 1963. CAF had already imposed a sporting ban on the apartheid state and were subsequently insulted and snubbed by FIFA in two further outlandish ways.

First, in order, as FIFA saw it, to avoid the embarrassment of dealing with South Africa in an African context, they placed the team in the Oceania/Asia qualifying group, along with Australia and North and South Korea. Second, FIFA cut a mind-boggling deal with South Africa. Should they qualify, they would be allowed to bring an all-white team to the 1966 finals. This was to be balanced, apparently, by the selection of an all-black team for 1970. This extraordinary 'solution' had emerged following a visit to South Africa by the then-president of FIFA, Stanley Rous, who expressed the fear that unless supported by his organisation, the very existence of football in South Africa was under threat. As it happened, the South Africans saved everyone a great deal of hand-wringing by failing to qualify.

This one-eyed emphasis on the importance of fostering relationships with white South Africa could not have been more out of tune with the force of pan-African nationalism that was taking root across the continent. In 1960, Kwame Nkrumah had assumed the presidency of newly independent Ghana. He was acutely aware of the strength of CAF as one of the few bodies at the time capable of speaking across nations. Having observed the pride fostered in Ghana's Black Stars, unofficial champions of Africa, Nkrumah saw international football as a viable and important political issue. 'Not only can sports contribute towards the development of unity and understanding between the regions of Ghana,' he suggested, 'they have another even more important role to play in present-day Africa ... through international competition with other African states, sports can provide that necessary basis of mutual understanding which can so greatly assist the realisation of our ideal of African unity.' The argument that the CAF was the organisational forerunner of the wider Organisation for African Unity, established with Nkrumah at its head in 1963, is a persuasive one.

The understandable anger of African nations at being treated so shabbily and their subsequent boycott, resulted in the truncated Asia and Oceania group being contested solely between both Koreas and Australia. With South Africa now banned, sort of for a bit, FIFA decided to play the qualifying tournament in Phnom Penh, Cambodia. For the impoverished, war-torn South Koreans, this was a logistical step too far and they were forced to withdraw. It all meant that in two matches over three days, and in front of healthy official attendances, North Korea despatched the Aussies 9-2 and were on their way to Middlesbrough. As champions, in effect, of Asia, Africa and Oceania.

Their campaign started with disappointment. The words of their newly commissioned anthem suggested that 'we can beat everyone, even the strongest team', but they were efficiently disposed of by the Soviet Union, 3-0, in front of an inquisitive crowd of just over 23,000 at Middlesbrough's Ayresome Park – the always dark and daunting forerunner of the anodyne Riverside Stadium. The curiosity about the Koreans is captured in the remarks of Middlesbrough fan Dennis Barry, who told the BBC that 'they played good football – you know they were all small and that was a novelty in itself – it was like watching a team of jockeys playing.' This appeal seemed to have diminished three days later when only 13,000 turned up to watch them play Chile, grabbing a late equaliser to earn themselves what turned out to be a valuable point. Four days after that, they had their own Belo Horizonte moment.

In their game against twice-champions Italy, Pak Doo-Ik scored a 42nd-minute goal entirely against the run of play and from there a combination of missed chances, heroic defending and splendid work by goalkeeper Lee Chang Myung meant that they held on for the unlikeliest of victories. Oh, and the fact that Italy played most of the game with ten men. In those pre-substitute days, their captain, Giacomo Bulgarelli, started the game with a knee injury that gave way in an early challenge. BBC commentator Frank Bough, who had observed during the Chile game that the Ayresome crowd 'don't cheer this loud for Middlesbrough', almost wept his reaction of 'they've won, they've won' into the microphone at the end of the game. North Korea had a place in the quarter-final.

Folklore reports that some 3,000 besotted Middlesbrough fans made their way to Goodison Park four days later to watch their adoptees take on Portugal, where a crowd of some 40,000 witnessed something quite extraordinary. Within half an hour, the Koreans were three up against the side that had burned through their previous group-stage opposition, including champions Brazil. In the subsequent 55 minutes, Portugal scored five goals, four of them from Eusebio da Silva Ferreira, always referred to by that single first name. He went on to win the Golden Boot for scoring the most goals in the tournament – nine – and won huge admiration for his conduct and sportsmanship, qualities on offer two years later during the European Cup Final where he played for Benfica against Manchester United at Wembley. He was one of the stars of the competition. And he was African – born into poverty in Mozambique in 1942. FIFA may have conspired to exclude African nations, but one of the darlings of the 1966 World Cup became a beloved standard-bearer for the continent.

The Koreans, with their speed and rapid passing, had brought a first indication to football's settled powers that they might not have the monopoly on how to play the game. It might have been that Eusebio's achievements made them take momentary stock about their relationship with Africa. Nevertheless, FIFA showed no intention of bestowing hosting favours beyond the usual suspects. In the 28 years that followed England's success, the finals alternated between the two main powers, Europe and South America, albeit with one genuine oddity.

In comparison to the circus of the modern bidding process, the selection of Mexico as hosts in 1970 looks like the raffle nobody cares about at the end of a social. Argentina was the only other country to submit a bid and were awarded the competition in 1978 for their efforts. Mexico had already demonstrated its logistical credentials by hosting the Olympics in 1968 and, besides, had something of an established footballing heritage. So their selection represented a departure from the two-pronged norm, but not one that was considered particularly outlandish. That is, until the World Cup returned there in 1986. And this time some very big political hitters were unapologetic about involving themselves in the world of the beautiful game.

In 1974, in a process with only one bidder, FIFA awarded the 1986 World Cup to Colombia. The film director Barbet Schroeder captures something of the hazy and dangerous nature of that country in his comment that it is 'hallucinatory, that's just the way everyday life is in Colombia – all the time you say to yourself, "Did I just see that?"' The activities of the Medellin drug cartel, undercover US destabilising operations, and the internecine turf warfare between the FARC, M19 and a host of other organisations, may have made good journalistic copy and generated masses of marketable folk-history, but 1980s Colombia was an international byword for instability and uncertainty. It came as no surprise, therefore, that hosting an SME, and a FIFA-led SME at that, became too burdensome. 'The 1986 world football championship will not be held in Colombia,' announced the country's president, Belisario Betancur, in October 1982, adding that, 'We have a lot of things to do here, and there is not enough time to attend to the extravagances of FIFA and its members.' Not, you may notice, the demands of football teams – 'FIFA and its members'.

The Colombian withdrawal meant that there were three prospective replacements: Canada, Mexico and the

United States. In May 1983, the three candidates were asked to make presentations to a special meeting of FIFA, chaired at that time by Joao Havelange. At the end of the process, with the award to Mexico confirmed, Havelange admitted to all present that 'there is no time for further postponement of our decision'. The delegations from the USA and Canada would have felt justifiably aggrieved. FIFA had sent an inspection team to Mexico but declined to do the same for either of the two other candidates. Nevertheless, Havelange, a Brazilian lawyer, felt comfortable in asserting that the process 'had been more than democratic'. Whatever other qualities he possessed, he was certainly not lacking nerve or fortitude: he was up against a formidable opponent, soaked in all the alleyway arts of political back-stabbery.

The United States delegation was headed by none other than Henry Albert Kissinger – the closest thing to a politically impermeable human being that has ever existed. In a career that spanned decades, he found himself charged with brokering peace following the Yom Kippur War in Israel, initiating détente with the USSR, opening relations between the USA and China and, in between times, engaging in shuttle diplomacy – it is suggested that this term originated from his energetic activities – from Pakistan to Chile to Turkey to Iran and Cyprus. He is (he's still alive at 98 as I write) a hugely divisive figure. Many regarded his policy decision to bomb Cambodia in 1970 as a war crime. When he was awarded the Nobel Peace Prize in 1973 for his part in ending the Vietnam War, the satirist Tom Lehrer famously wrote that it marked the end of political satire. For all of this, he was, and remains, one of the most prominent figures in the modern era of US politics. None of which prepared him for dealing with FIFA.

He admitted to the *New York Times* that his advocacy had been 'dismally unsuccessful' and that the 'politics of soccer make me nostalgic for the politics of the Middle East'. He went on to observe, almost wistfully, that the bid had 'the backing of our president and a unanimous Congress, which is more than President Reagan usually can achieve.' Kissinger may well have stood astride the world of global politics, but FIFA's highly honed sense of its own infallibility rendered him a frustrated and unsuccessful bystander.

Its movements may have been arthritic, but FIFA was surveying a changing landscape – all the while calculating potential profit. When Diego Maradona's deified hands held the trophy aloft in the Estadio Azteca on 29 June 1986, it marked the second competition that had accommodated 24 rather than 16 teams in the final stages. Wikipedia may have manifold faults as a source of information, but it is instructive to look through its entries for successive World Cups. These all begin with an initial paragraph concerning host selection, with issues around some sort of political chicanery forming the bulk of the section. Yet, for it all, the hosting stranglehold of Europe and South America was loosening and participation was widening. By the time of the 1998 tournament in France, the number of teams had expanded to 32, with 15 teams from Europe and five from South America – the same number as from Africa and one more from Asia. The United States had already held the competition four years earlier, and in 2002 the roadshow was setting off for Japan and South Korea. In 2010 the hosts would be South Africa, with, no doubt, the spirit of Sir Stanley Rous smiling on benignly from beyond the stars.

In 1966, English attitudes to the participation of the North Koreans reflected the dominant ideas of a post-war society not quite ready to come to terms with the gradual fading of its imperial past. How curious it was that people beyond the established 'footballing nations' should even know how to play so well, never mind bring a different set of skills to the game. Might there even be other countries out there playing football that we don't even know about? Chinamen, maybe? People down in deepest Africa? While it is easy to sneer at such narrow thinking from a distance of half a century, the extent to which the past is a different country is difficult to overstate. A good place to start to get a sense of this is on TV.

The best estimate of the accounting mega-company KPMG is that the broadcasting of the 2018 World Cup in Russia generated something in the region of £6bn from selling rights to advertisers and broadcasters. The game's TV reach extended to 217 countries across Africa, the Americas, Europe, Asia and Oceania. It is now indisputable that for the World Cup and for all top-level football, the game exists for TV. Whether that manifests itself in the vainglorious attempt to establish super-leagues, or on the more mundane level of the fan who loses the pre-booked train deal because his Championship team's game has been moved to the Sunday lunchtime graveyard slot (apologies for introducing personal pain here), TV rules the footballing roost in the form of live matches, highlights packages and the lucrative world of console games. Football on the screen far outweighs its presence on grass as far as the game's financial directors are concerned.

In April 1962, Peter Dimmock, the general manager of the BBC, signed the TV deal with FIFA for £300,000. There was a stipulation between FIFA and the BBC that any overlapping of matches should be kept to a minimum. Grounds were to be thoroughly inspected to ensure that camera and commentary positions were suitable and, for the first time, the miracle of the slow-motion replay was to be available for some games. 'In every soccer competition,' gushed the *Radio Times*, 'there is always something that happens so quickly that not even the sharpest and most experienced of observers can be exactly sure of what took place.'

With England reaching the final, Dimmock must have been overjoyed at overseeing this moment of televised national triumph. *The Times* suggested that he and his associates 'must be preening themselves at their own world record on Saturday afternoon – four hundred million viewers in four, or was it five, continents were transfixed to their tellies watching twenty-two footballers'. Lest the significance be lost on its readership, they were reminded that 'the last occasion when viewing on this world scale went on was during the funeral of a true world statesman, Churchill'.

Global TV coverage, huge screens in town squares and nations grinding to a halt to watch their teams' exploits are now all central parts of football's SME. When, in pre-pandemic times, it was possible to be present in such places, the moving wallpaper in any bar from China to Vietnam to Oman displayed non-stop action from the world's (more usually Europe's) football glamour clubs. To observe that football is a business, and a global, multi-billion-dollar one, is to state nothing more than the obvious. The lost world of jolly, little Koreans having a go at playing football has evaporated and the centre of the footballing map on the wall is no longer obviously located in Europe or South America. Everybody, it seems, loves football and plenty more love the cash it generates. The idea that emergent, ambitious nations wouldn't want a slice of the cake is as outdated as the dominant red on the map of Empire.

The notion of a New World Order has exercised geopolitical thinking since the end of the Cold War, meaning different things to different people with different axes to grind. It is one that has moved centre-stage as war on our doorstep is beamed into our living rooms. As far as football is concerned, its newer kids on the block may not yet have become champions, but when it comes to the strategic game of hosting, they've proved themselves adept learners. We should be cautious before we carelessly dismiss Qatar's success as just more run-of-the-mill slimy practice and what would you expect from that part of the world, anyway? Maybe they did some looking and learning of their own. 'If we are like you in the rest, we will resemble you in that,' says Shylock to his tormentors, meaning that behaviours, good and bad, can be learnt from dominant powers. Put another way, we had plenty of rubbish stuffed in our own cupboards to make the place look tidy.

In August 2012, former US attorney Michael J Garcia was appointed by FIFA to investigate any breaches of ethical conduct in relation to the awards of the 2018 and 2022 World Cups. We'll be looking at his efforts in some detail in the next chapter. In the meantime, however, glimpses into Garcia's commentary on the conduct of England's FA is horribly uncomfortable. Among his concerns is that Trinidad's Jack Warner, now banned from all football activities since 2015, used his position to 'shower England's bid team with inappropriate requests' in return for support for his vote for the 2018 competition. Garcia concluded that 'England 2018's response shows an unfortunate willingness, time and again, to meet that expectation'. Warner's request that the England bid team find employment in the English game for the teenage son of his personal banker resulted in 'consultancies' for the young man at both Tottenham and Aston Villa. Leaving aside important questions as to whether these are suitable workplaces for any young person, it's a sharp reminder that clean hands are a rarity when the stakes are high. In the murky world of World Cup bidding, there are no good guys; just villains of varying degrees of awfulness. As Garcia's report revealed all too clearly …

Chapter 5

It's going to be a scorcher out there, but don't fret. Money will make it all fine

FIFA'S 38-PAGE document evaluating Qatar's bid for the 2022 World Cup isn't riveting stuff. It dutifully trawls through its observations about stadia, transport links, airport connections, associated legal insurance cover and all levels of risk that need to be considered. Written in plain, unemotive and unambiguous prose, it does exactly what it should – presents an objective account of what the FIFA delegation inspected, what questions and issues arose from their scrutiny and finishes with a bland, largely non-committal set of conclusions. Any of us condemned to trawl through such reports for professional purposes will be familiar with its dull, but necessary, conformity. 'We feel we have accomplished our work in the spirit of integrity, objectiveness and transparency,' writes Harold Mayne-Nicholls, the chairman (yep, not chair) of the Evaluation Committee in his introduction. Well, fair enough. Are you still awake out there?

On the face of it, there seems to be much to like about the bid. Although most of the stadia weren't built at the time it was submitted, there is a commitment to staging a carbon-neutral event through the deployment of environmentally friendly cooling techniques. Moreover, after the event, 22 modular sections of the yet-to-be-built stadia were to be used to construct facilities around the world, encouraging the growth of the game in Thailand, Nepal, Nigeria and Pakistan. The bid promises to use the Qatar event as the basis for developing the women's game in the Middle East and points to its success in hosting the 1995 Under-20 World Cup as proof of its commitment to bringing the game to young people. In terms of box-ticking, it's a thorough piece of work and is acknowledged as such by the evaluators.

The Qatari bidders see much of the strength of their work residing in the compactness of the area designed to incorporate stadia, hotels, training camps and FIFA's headquarters (oh yes, FIFA's headquarters – of course). Doha airport will be expanded and new transport links will be in place. Hotel capacity will be increased once a substantial building programme gets under way. It's worth a pause here for a moment.

As I write, practically every major infrastructure programme in the UK is failing. Nobody knows where HS2 is now going or when it might get there. Crossrail in London seems to have been under construction since before reliable records began and the much-needed NHS IT programme is still bumping helplessly along the bottom. We've then had the utter fiasco of awarding various Covid-related contracts to people so unutterably incompetent that they were even incapable of kicking over the traces of their own misdemeanours. In short, we have become accustomed to things simply not getting done. Not so in Qatar, at least in the judgement of the evaluating committee.

'The decision-making process in the country,' it observes, 'offers certain advantages in terms of the implementation of events and operations.' Quite. There are definite advantages to bypassing pesky democratic processes. Therefore, the committee concludes, when it comes, for example, to the construction of hotel rooms, they can be content that 'the Qatari government guarantees FIFA that the construction and availability of rooms' will all be delivered, even though this guarantee is 'based on interventions that do not yet exist'. Nowhere is this reliance on things that only exist in the imagination of the bidders more evident than in the two-page spread depicting the 12 potential stadia. (There will, in fact, be eight in use in 2022.) Looking like a collection resembling everything between exotic sea-creatures, spaceships and, just occasionally, a plain old football ground, nine of these sporting temples did not exist and those that did would require major renovation. But, apparently, it'd all get done. The proposed stadia all 'appear to fulfil FIFA … space and quality requirements' and the evaluators appear relaxed about the availability of the $3bn dollars needed to bring this about. But they do have a small worry.

June and July in Qatar are warm. A chart in the document shows average temperatures hovering around 40°C at noon and dropping only to about 36°C at 4pm. Other sources indicate that daytime temperatures of 46°C are common: on the playing surfaces in the middle of enclosed stands, they could approach 50°C. Once again, FIFA seems relaxed. 'Barring unforeseen epidemics or developments' – and there won't be any of those any time soon, will there? – 'there is no major risk in staging the event in this country.' This seems somewhat at odds with a comment just a few lines later which notes that playing football in Qatar in the two hottest months of the year poses 'a potential health risk for players, spectators, officials and the FIFA family in both open training sites and in stadiums' and would necessitate the taking of special precautions such as hydration schemes, sun shields, ice, cooling mists and cooling breaks. And once more, FIFA trusts that such measures will be firmly in place, otherwise why draw the conclusion that their 'requirements for health and international standards are likely to be met'?

In their summary of risk assessment, the evaluators only identify one high-risk area, which is the installation and efficiency of various cooling systems that do not yet exist. They're happy about the timings of TV transmissions, content about the legal basis of the bid, confident that buildings and infrastructure will all be jobs that get done – it's just the playing of the football in one of the hottest places on the planet that's the problem. It's a perfect example of the game at top level in the modern age. It reveals the gaping discrepancy between football as a marketable commodity and the pastime that connects kids kicking a ball in the park to their commodified heroes, forever under public gaze.

We know now that the stadia were built and that the cooling systems are in place. And we know, too, that the games won't be played in high summer but will cut across a multitude of national leagues. But when it came to playing in the inferno, it didn't take long for the eyebrows of some of the game's grandees to be raised.

Almost immediately, one of the game's biggest names put his hat in the ring. Franz Beckenbauer, the Kaiser, suggested that 'it might be better to think about another solution', such as playing the matches in January or February when temperatures would be no more challenging than those endured in parts of Brazil or the

USA. In an age where the appropriation of self-appointed titles – The Guv'nor, The Boss – abound in sporting circles at all levels, there's nothing vainglorious about Beckenbauer's adopted title. Quite simply, there had never been anything like him. Maybe England's elegant Bobby Moore had made us think that centre-halves (for that's what they were) didn't necessarily have to be big blokes who did headers, no-nonsense clearances and bone-crunching tackles. But Beckenbauer was something entirely new.

Here was a bloke who would put in the tackle that his position required and then not just pick a perfect pass to a team-mate. No such simple option for him. He would start running forward with the ball! What was he playing at? Off past the halfway line he would go, head held high as he surveyed the possibilities around him before offloading the ball and then, in one in seven occasions for both club and country, go on to score. He was, quite simply, utterly majestic. When it turned out that he'd been unable to keep his fingers out of the dirty money swamp that gurgles around everything connected to FIFA, those of us who had watched him with awe – even down to making hilariously stumbling efforts to be him on rutted parks' pitches – could only sigh at the venal way of the world.

Beckenbauer had headed up Germany's successful bid for the 2006 World Cup and, almost by default one imagines, found himself in the world of wheeler-dealing that ends up, literally, with bungs being handed over in plain envelopes. At the bottom of this grimy saga is the Kaiser's association with the Qatari Mohammed bin Hammam, former FIFA executive committee member, once president of the Asian Football Confederation and now banned from football for life twice over. The footballer, along with Wolfgang Niersbach and Theo Zwanziger, still remains accused of handing some £8m (estimates vary) to Bin Hammam in horse-trading for votes for hosting. Bin Hammam, in turn, was found to have paid over sums in wads of notes up to £20,000 each time to the serially greedy beggar Jack Warner from Trinidad. When asked by the German broadcaster ZDF in 2018 if the money from Beckenbauer and his associates was a bribe, Bin Hammam responded, 'I don't know … but excuse me, it's only you who cares, no one else.' Such blunt reticence resulted in Bin Hammam's irretrievable ban. But what of Beckenbauer?

It turns out that for him and his associates from the German bid team, Covid was an ill-wind that blew them some good. In April 2020 his case was to be heard by a newly reconstituted FIFA council in Zurich, some 15 years since the first allegations were made against him. With a Swiss statute of limitations in place that prevented cases being heard once those 15 years had elapsed, the Kaiser once again slipped effortlessly past those who were trying to tackle him and emerged cool, unscathed and smiling as proceedings were postponed. FIFA reacted by announcing, 'The fact that the case has now ended without a result of any kind is very worrying, not only for football but also for the administration of justice in Switzerland.' Some people might just think that an organisation that had conducted its own affairs with a cavalier disregard for ethical conduct commenting on the judiciary processes of a nation state might just be a touch, well, impertinent. But thoughtful introspection has never seemed high on the list of priorities of football's overlords.

Nevertheless, when it came to playing football in the desert sun, Beckenbauer was not on his own when voicing concern. FIFA's chief medical officer, Belgian Michel D'Hooghe, was quick to raise his anxieties. It seems to be a rule that anyone connected to FIFA must have at least a few bones, if not an entire skeleton, lurking somewhere. It turns out that D'Hooghe's medical expertise had already been put to the test in the world of international football.

In 2007, D'Hooghe had expressed his professional view that the wearing of headscarves by women footballers presented dangers from both strangulation and overheating. Reporting on the issue is scant, but once he pedalled back from this judgement, the accredited quotes from D'Hooghe take some fathoming. 'The problems I had [with scarves] were medical and I don't have those problems any more,' he explained, before going on to say, 'There is no risk of strangulation – I was asked for a medical opinion and the discussions I had were purely medical.' This change of heart seemed to arise as the result of a concerted challenge to this medical opinion led by Prince Ali of Jordan, who, according to reports, had located medical research that challenged D'Hooghe's view.

I have no wish to cast any aspersions on his majesty's academic ability, but any such medical research must be very well hidden. There is in abundance of research carried out by academics from around the world. The work of Jordanian Manal Hamzeh is in the forefront of this, and it characterizes the apparent concerns about hijab-wearing footballers as being culturally, rather than medically, driven. When pressed on his reasons for changing his medical view, there is no recorded comment from D'Hooghe.

None of which should overshadow one enormously significant contribution that D'Hooghe has made to the game and that has benefited footballers from Hackney Marshes to the Maracana. Some 50 years ago, in attendance at his local club, FC Brugge, D'Hooghe, a newly qualified doctor, ran onto the pitch to give mouth-to-mouth resuscitation to Nico Rijnders, a young Dutch player. By a curious quirk of fate, Rijnders had come through the Ajax youth scheme in the same way as Christian Eriksen, whose sudden cardiac arrest on the field of play was witnessed by millions during Euro 2020. The incident with Rijnders – who regrettably died of congenital heart failure three years after D'Hooghe's actions had saved him on the pitch – made a lasting impression on the young doctor. He established a rehabilitation centre in Bruges for footballers with unexpected heart conditions and then set about ensuring that clubs and associations the world over invested in defibrillators and heart-monitoring equipment. Above all, his campaigning raised awareness about the vulnerability of young, fit athletes to cardiac arrest. It's a telling contribution.

For all of this, D'Hooghe couldn't simply enjoy the reputational success brought on by this particular piece of sound clinical advice. For reasons that only he could explain, he accepted a 'small painting' in 2011 from one of the members of the Russian bid team for 2018. When challenged about it, he said it was a 'poisonous gift' that was worth next to nothing. His son also acquired a medical post in Qatar and, once again, D'Hooghe was insistent that this had nothing to do with his involvement with FIFA. Insinuations of any impropriety prompted him to tell media outlets that he was 'simply a man who has worked for years and years trying to improve medical issues at FIFA' and that he was heartily aggrieved at being 'considered a murderer'. And he possibly had a case. A humane and persuasive conversation with a Middle

Eastern prince, a water colour of antelope on the steppes and a clever offspring who secured, under his own steam, a decent job in a well-equipped hospital. All of these are perfectly proper, feasible and honest episodes. It's just that if you work with FIFA, there's some muck about somewhere and everybody believes that some of it has to rub off on you.

By March 2015, even FIFA's obtuseness about playing in the oven had been punctured. The concerns of legends of the game and informed medical opinion had made their impression, because a FIFA task force met and discussed the probability of moving the competition to the winter months. The broadcasting gods had already decreed that January and February of 2022 would be out of the question because of the Winter Olympics in Beijing. US companies were wary of anything that might cut across major winter sports, particularly NFL – American football – in November and December. Yet it was these months that FIFA, working in conjunction with the Qatar bid team, identified as the most likely solution. How to deal with these various conundrums?

Once Qatar had been awarded the World Cup, it hadn't taken long for the initial contracts on rights to be drawn up. The main companies outside Europe – Fox, Telemundo and Futbol de Primera – were quick to seal a deal in the region of $1.2bn, sharply and efficiently hoovering up access to the action. FIFA's general secretary,

Jerome Valcke, was a happy boy. 'FIFA is delighted with the progress of our media rights sale to date which, coming amid austere economic times, more than confirm the strength and appeal of our competitions.' But what about Fox and Telemundo, broadcasting mainly to the Americas? Would November or June really make any difference to them?

The time difference between the east coast of the USA and Qatar is seven hours: from Rio it is six. Should enthusiasts from the Americas wish to watch a game that kicks off in mid-afternoon or late evening in the Middle East, it could prove a diverting accompaniment to a late breakfast, morning coffee or lunch. Would it make much difference if this happened in the depths of winter or in the middle of summer, particularly if your team was playing? It's difficult to see why it might, although work and school schedules might just play a part. What it wouldn't do was cut across the schedule of home-based sports. But Fox, having already shelled out early to broadcast the event, wasn't quite so relaxed.

In an emailed memo to FIFA in September 2013, the company irritably pointed out that it had been brought to their attention that there may be moves afoot to move the 2022 event to the winter. 'Fox Sports bought the World Cup rights with the understanding that [matches] would be in the summer as they have been since they have been since the 1930s.' While it's good to know that the Fox corporation guards the history and traditions of the game with such integrity, it's difficult to know what their beef would have been. No matches would be scheduled at the same time as NFL or anything else being played on the entire continent. It turns out that it wasn't the change that bothered them: what they really wanted to do was make a fuss and look like they'd been hard done by.

And it worked. Two years after their grizzling email, Fox (and Telemundo) were granted the rights for the 2026 competition scheduled for the USA, Canada and Mexico. No tendering process was required. Whatever the Fox executives had cooked up behind the scenes had worked its magic. Its principal competitors, ESPN and Univision, had been frozen out of a process that netted FIFA a sum just under $500,000 – an amount they boasted they could have doubled had the rights been put out to open competition. Nonetheless, the gravy train of sponsorship and advertising hadn't even begun to poke its head out of the sidings: there'd be plenty more noughts to add to these early figures. With the 2026 competition expanding to 48 teams in the finals, the money-makers were already gearing up for a feeding frenzy. Media consultant Lee Berke told Bloomberg News that Fox's success meant that the World Cup coverage was 'going to be as strong a ratings force as you can possibly have for a sports property'. A sports property. I'll just leave that there.

Did the Qataris or FIFA ever seriously think that matches would be played in July? It's impossible to know. What we can be more sure about is that even if playing in such heat had ever been considered an obstacle, there must have been a confidence – which certainly wasn't misplaced – that powerful money would find a solution. As we'll see in later chapters, the potential knock-on effect on the world's major leagues, in both 2022 and beyond, could turn out to be massively significant.

What about the workers who would make this miracle occur? We'll come to them just as soon as we've looked at what happened at Qatar's World Cup dress rehearsal.

Chapter 6

Meanwhile, in December in Doha, a proper football tournament. Politics-free? Don't you believe it

IN EARLY December 2021, while the TV companies tried to convince us that dead rubbers of the Champions League really were worth watching or, with committed fans being excusable exceptions, that we needed to take an interest in the dying gasps of the Europa League's group stages, a real-life football tournament was taking place in Qatar. It was the tenth Arab Cup and the first to bear the imprimatur of FIFA. Their website took pride in announcing that 'the event offers a great opportunity for competitors and spectators alike to experience the spirit of Qatar and the iconic stadiums [of course they're iconic, what other adjective to use for football grounds?] that will host the World Cup in 2022'. It may not have registered on the consciousness of many, possibly because, unlike the Africa Cup of Nations, Premier League stars had not committed to turning out for their country for this one. Nevertheless, it was a competition that had a lot to put on show, piquing interest for what was to come.

Whittled down to 16 teams for the final stages and played between the last day of November and 18 December, its highest-ranked nation was Tunisia (26th) and the lowest Sudan (124th). Along the way Comoros (no, me neither, but we'll hear of then again later on), Yemen, Kuwait, South Sudan and Djibouti had been eliminated in qualifiers. In the group stages, the hosts breezed through with maximum points, having brushed away Oman, Iraq and Bahrain. Relative heavyweights Morocco and Tunisia topped their groups, although the latter only on goal difference. It was Group D that provided the needle, the fireworks, some VAR (of course) and even the potential for a bit of traditional football-match romance for the big screen.

From that group, Egypt and Algeria, the current African champions, had both qualified by the time they met on 7 December in the Al Janoub Stadium in Al Wakrah, 15 miles south of Doha. Notwithstanding the advertisers' insistence on slapping images of Mohamed Salah on anything remotely connected with the game, the Liverpool striker remained miles from the desert, focussing, no doubt, on the weekend's upcoming fixture against the Villa. He'll have been glad to have missed what turned out to be a bit of rumble.

Unlike many of the group games, the crowd was large, raucous and, unlike what could be gleaned from some of the footage, very largely male. The two teams went into the tie with identical records: two wins, six goals scored, none conceded and crucially, given its criterion as potential tie-breaker, the same number of disciplinary points. It's fair to say that they both went to it with a will from the start. Twenty minutes in, Algeria took the lead when Mohamed Tougai benefited from some penalty-box pinball to score. He then balanced this effort by giving away a clumsy penalty on the hour, necessitating a ref-to-TV decision, with the resultant kick scored by Amr El Solia. As the game drifted into added-on time and with the 1-1 draw providing no distinguishing feature between their records, there was nothing to separate the two teams.

Earlier in the game, 18-year-old Algerian Yacine Titraoui had been booked for a routine but clumsy challenge. He then managed to use some professional nous, notwithstanding his youth, to keep out of trouble … until the 94th minute. With the referee's whistle all but poised to blow for time, Mohanad Lishen brought the ball away from Egypt's penalty area only for young Titraoui to commit to an airborne lunge in true Sunday ale-house fashion to earn himself an unnecessarily hilarious red card. Given the grievous nature of the assault, the need for the referee once again to trot over to the pitchside TV to upgrade an originally lenient yellow seemed a touch peculiar, but there'd be no appealing this particular decision. His flying stab at his opponent's shin – well worth a moment to check out online – meant that his team had to settle for second place and a game against Morocco. There was a strong feeling that the two teams would meet again in the final, but Tunisia's victory over Egypt in the quarter-final soon put paid to that.

Qatar was very sensibly using the Arab Cup as a rehearsal for staging the real thing. Although its coverage was somewhat bland, the official government website made the Cup headline news, superseded only by information about the need to combat Covid. One has to imagine that transport systems, logistics and stadium management were all being trialled as the tournament progressed, even if the crowds themselves would have been largely made up of expats, for whom hotel accommodation would not have been a significant requirement. Broadcasters, too, were honing their skills of manipulating crowd reaction. TV camera operators at SMEs everywhere on the planet have obviously not yet received the memo that finding a pretty girl and lingering for just that nanosecond too long is not a compulsory part of the 21st-century telecast. But in one traditional area, they still missed a trick.

The day after Titraoui's ugly thresh, the *Doha News* ran the headline 'Newlyweds celebrate wedding at Algeria v Egypt FIFA Arab Cup match.' Just as a very brief aside, I'm in no position to sneer here. Five days after my own wedding in December 1982, I took my new bride to Birmingham v Villa at St Andrew's. I attribute our 3-0 victory to her presence and we've remained firmly united since. The couple at the Al Janoub preferred to remain anonymous, but the bride, pictured in the story, informed the paper that she'd 'always wanted to come to Qatar and my husband told me that as soon as I land in Qatar, we'll celebrate our marriage ... and, oh, we'll be able to catch a game at the same time as well. Great, eh?' I put that last bit in myself. The TV crew had failed to capture the couple during the action and so one can only imagine that there would have been a debrief at some point about the importance of capturing any weddings and, even more crucially, any staged marriage proposals in future.

Meanwhile the host nation continued to make sparkling progress, much to the delight, no doubt, of organisers and advertisers throughout the nation. In their first knockout game, they thrilled a crowd of over 63,000 in the Al Bayt stadium by putting five past the UAE before the half-time whistle and then settling down, as sides so often do, to an exercise in tame game management for the remainder of the contest. I say 'thrilled' and I convey the official attendance, but frankly, my dear, I'm not entirely convinced of either.

Given its relative invisibility to most European media and those TV stations which somehow manage to locate some football – any football – to fill their schedules, the action in the Arab Cup was only readily available on FIFA's own site. Here, the committed addict could either watch games in their entirety or catch up with the neatly edited highlights packages that appeared on the website soon after matches had finished. These short broadcasts were slick and clear and benefited from informed and knowledgeable English commentary. But there were a couple of tell-tale queries.

To explain. I have only a passing interest in *Match of the Day* as it's been ten years since my team appeared on it – and even then, we were often condemned to the weary final-game slot. I usually record it on Saturday night and buzz through it, minus interviews and analysis, while munching my cereal on Sunday morning. I have no statistical analysis to validate the claim that follows, but I do know that this is probably a habit I share with, quite possibly, tens of thousands of people. My other guilty-ish footballing pleasure is watching the League One and Two goals show on Sky. Much of the entertainment derived from this is remarking – usually to myself – that that's where that useless lump is playing now or, in my case, smugly ticking off the ground as one that I've been to. I appreciate, on reading back those last few sentences, that I have painted a sorry, but probably quite accurate, portrait of myself. That, however, is not the purpose of invoking the lower-league goal-fest programme. It's the broadcaster's manipulation of crowd noise that is as hilarious as it is unbelievable.

The sound editors ask us to believe that the brave assembly of away fans, clumped under the tin roof of the least attractive part of the ground, emit a noise equivalent to a gathering of 20 times their number, with this uproar echoing through an acoustically designed stadium around them. Now if there's one thing I know about, it's about being in a few tinpot away ends. I also know – and I've written about this elsewhere – that the joy and delight of your team scoring, which always, incidentally, comes as a surprise to me, can prompt unbridled, almost animalistic, vocal reaction. What it doesn't sound like, though, is the wild, roaring appreciation from the Maracana or the Nou Camp. But this deception on the part of the sound engineers is part of the imperative of footballing broadcasting which states that everything simply has to be FANTASTIC. Even when it's not. Put simply, the crowd noise on FIFA's site was at odds with the ocular proof.

Much of this revealed large swathes of empty seating, particularly in upper tiers of the stadium. At first glance this seems even more pronounced, with vast ranks of unbroken white sections in the crowd, until it becomes clear that these are massed tiers of spectators wearing white thawbs – traditional male Arab dress – topped off with keffiyehs. When goals are scored, the camera operators' immediate attention is divided between pretty girls – see above – and these gentlemen. Typically, the former are taking snaps on their phone and the latter are cheering somewhat decorously while happily, but demurely, jigging about a bit. There is no possible way that the noise emitted from the video clip is commensurate with the reactions of those who are, supposedly, generating it.

When it comes to the official attendance figures, once again it's kind of comforting that the super-duper media machine of the late internet era has plenty in common with dodgy turnstile operators, and even dodgier club owners, of yesteryear. Regular match-goers, who know what their ground looks like when it's either full or, more typically, at its patchy Tuesday best, ritually exchange japes about the announcement of the gate, speculating on the honesty of impending tax returns. The official pre-tournament capacity for the Al Bayt is 60,000: the gate for the Qatar UAE game is recorded at an official 63,439 – which, given the empty upper tiers, might have indicated an alarming health and safety situation.

Which is probably the exact opposite of what happened. For all the dubious but familiar bits of fiddling, FIFA and the Qatari authorities could happily congratulate themselves on a perfectly satisfactory dress rehearsal for the main event. Regrettably for those in the hosts' camp, they failed to make it to the final, losing to Algeria to a dramatic goal, scored when their keeper could only push the ball back to Youcef Belaili, who had just fluffed his penalty kick, in the 17th minute of time added on. Not extra time; time added on because of VAR and the fact that Qatar themselves had pinched what they thought was their own dramatic equalizer in the 97th minute. They at least had the scant consolation of grabbing third place in the competition by beating Egypt, who had fallen at the hands of Tunisia in the other semi-final.

So it was that on 18 December, Qatar's national day, that Tunisia and Algeria faced each other in the final at the Al Bayt (official attendance, 60,456). Exactly a year to the day after the event, the World Cup final itself is scheduled to take place. 'It's the Maghreb derby,' enthused the commentator, taking his cue from those who insist on manufacturing ridiculous notions like the 'M69 derby' (Coventry v Leicester. Really) or the equally preposterous Brighton v Palace confection. Your grounds are 46 miles apart. Forty-six.

And if this was, indeed, a derby, it was a tepid affair in comparison to the blood and thunder of Algeria's earlier clash with Egypt. Goalless at full time, substitute Amir Sayoud then caressed an exquisite left-footer past

Tunisia's Hassen Mouez ten minutes into extra time. In the siege that followed, Tunisia forced a corner in the final minute. Mouez came up for it, the ball was cleared to Yacine Brahimi in the centre circle who then had nothing other to do than escort the ball, with no other player in sight, into the Tunisian box before belting it into the empty net to definitively win the game. Leaving Algeria to go and collect the cup.

With the handshakes finished and the medals duly distributed, the regulation bunny-jumping and hugging on the victors' podium ensues. Fireworks explode, music blares and the cup is held aloft. Flags are draped in various styles around waists or fashioned into cloaks. Two flags are in evidence. The first, unsurprisingly, is that of Algeria. The second is that of Palestine. It's far from being the first time that it has assumed such prominence during the competition.

The opening ceremony was the first indication of the depth of support for Palestine, with its team receiving as enthusiastic a reception as that of the hosts. Despite only managing a single point from their three group stage games, the Palestinians were clearly the neutrals' favourites in all these contests. Such support was never clearer than when Algeria played Morocco at the Al Thumama in the quarter finals. Level at 2-2 after extra time, Algeria won the penalty shoot-out to go through. As the players raced across the pitch in celebration, it was the Palestinian flag that was most in evidence. If the needle on the pitch hadn't matched up to the game against Egypt, the Moroccans could not have failed to feel the rebuke in this gesture from their opponents.

In one of the last acts of the Trump presidency, the Moroccan government in Rabat had been persuaded to normalise diplomatic relationships with Israel. They had done so in exchange for US support in their claim to sovereignty over parts of the Western Sahara region. Seen as collusion and treachery, the hashtag 'normalisation is treachery' trended around the Arab world. Condemned as 'foreign manoeuvres which aim to destabilise Algeria,' by Prime Minister Abdelaziz Djerad, the actions of Rabat and the US were characterised as 'a desire by the Zionist entity to come close to our borders'. As Youcef Balaili, the scorer of Algeria's second goal with a spectacular 45-yard strike, careered across the turf in Doha flourishing Palestine's flag after the Morocco game, he was being cheered to the rafters in Ramallah and Gaza City as well as Algiers. Defender Houcine Benayada told reporters, 'We do not play for any bonus, we play for these two flags.' His comments were amplified by coach Madjid Bougherra, who dedicated the victory to the people of Palestine and 'to the Gaza Strip in particular'.

This unremitting support for Palestine had an echo in most, if not all, of the Arab world. One other exception was the government of the UAE, which underwent similar opprobrium to that of Morocco for its opening of diplomatic relations with Israel. Its manifestation at the Arab Cup would not have come as any surprise to anyone. Journalist Tagreed al-Armour explained, 'Algerian support in football for Palestine has always drawn attention to the need for continued Arab support for the right to self-determination for Palestine and for the end of the Israeli occupation – those who crown their victory with the Palestine flags and the keffiyeh are doing so to send the message of one blood, a symbol of Arab unity, and a rejection of colonialism and normalisation.'

This sustained message of solidarity, augmented with such public vigour by the winners of the tournament, would, one imagines, have caused few flutterings in the corridors of Qatari power. Earlier in the year, as a handful of Arab states resumed diplomatic relationships with Israel, foreign minister Mohammed bin Abdulrahman Al Thani made it clear that this was not something that was on the cards as far as Qatar was concerned. The main reason, he reminded a press conference, that we don't have relations with Israel 'is the occupation of Palestine territories'. Clear and unequivocal. The question that arises, however, is just how relaxed he and his colleagues would have been when witnessing the unapologetic political messaging coming from the Algerians and other participants. And what would FIFA say?

FIFA, with its beautifully appointed offices, its teams of lawyers, its army of consultants, its access to the thoughts and ideas of some of the best players of the game and its global reach? What does FIFA have to say about the perennially contentious issue of politics and football? You want a straightforward answer? From FIFA? You haven't been paying attention, have you?

To be fair, the wording of their rulings is plain, explaining that neither players' equipment nor their undergarments should display materials 'that show political, religious, personal slogans, statements or images, or advertising other than the manufacturer's logo'. Heaven forbid that they should fail to put that on display. The ruling goes on to warn, 'For any offence, the player and/or the team will be sanctioned by the competition organiser, national football association or by FIFA.' But as is so often the case with the masters of the world game, such apparent clarity takes only moments to become obscured in the fog of compromise, expediency and muddled inconsistency.

This isn't a surprise, of course. The Law in Sport organisation captures FIFA's immediate predicament with a neat piece of understatement. It explains that football can't wash itself clean of the taint of political involvement because 'the governance of football itself appears to be so political that nothing can alter this perception'. It amplifies this by observing that it 'is hard at times as an observer to see how FIFA can advocate that football remains apolitical when as an organisation ... its own lines appear to be less clear'. A glance at its track record would seem to confirm this lack of clarity.

In 2013 it fined Croatia's Josip Simunic £20,000 for his action in orchestrating a pro-fascist chant among supporters in Zagreb, following victory against Iceland in a World Cup qualifier. As well as the fine, FIFA imposed a hefty ban on Simunic, effectively ruling him out of participation in the finals in Brazil. An official statement explained that 'after taking into account all of the circumstances of the case, and particularly given the gravity of the incident, the committee decided to suspend the player for ten official matches'. Some months later, the Argentinian team unfurled a banner prior to a friendly with Slovenia, proclaiming, 'Las Malvinas son Argentinas' – the Falklands belong to Argentina. FIFA imposed the same £20,000 ban on the Argentine federation as they had on Simunic alone. Despite this disparity in financial penalties, FIFA's stance seemed to be clear enough. As a spokesman for the International Football Association Board, Jonathan Ford of the Welsh FA explained, 'To determine what is right and wrong between different countries and cultures is very complicated, so it's easier to say it's got no place in the game.'

Which seems to be a simple, if disingenuously optimistic, approach. In 2016, FIFA handed out a more substantial fine to the English FA – £35,000 – for allowing players to wear the poppy symbol on their official kit. Similar, slightly smaller fines were handed out to the associations of Wales, Scotland and Northern Ireland. Prime Minister Theresa May was predictably outraged. 'Our football players want to recognise and respect those who have given their lives for our safety and security,' she said. 'I think it is absolutely right that they should be able to do so.' Predictably, the online comments section of the *Daily Mail* was roiling with fury: FIFA was 'a bunch of low life pond scum', 'corrupt' and 'so out of touch'. The notion that it was an organisation that should put its own house in order before fixing its attention on others was a recurring theme.

There must have been some scurrying about in corridors of FIFA's power when, a few weeks after the fine for the poppy-wearing, someone must have spotted footage of the Republic of Ireland's game against Switzerland in Dublin back in March. The Irish team had sported badges commemorating 100 hundred years since the Easter Rising against British rule. Sharp-eyed Conservative MP Damian Collins was on the case. 'I have asked FIFA to clarify the issue over shirts worn by the Republic of Ireland because that appears to be an absolutely classic example of leniency being shown to other countries,' he told the BBC. And whether it was the intervention of the Right Honourable Gentleman or just a case of some hurried retrospective justice, FIFA duly imposed a fine of just under £5,000 on the Irish FA.

I can find no recorded reaction from Josip Suminic to this apparent leniency. He currently earns his living as the coach of Croatia's under-19s team and, it seems, still takes an active interest in right-wing – very right-wing – politics. He has been an active campaigner for the adoption of militaristic insignia on the shirt of the national team and has been a financial patron of a documentary denying Croatian involvement in massacres of Jews and Serbs in the Second World War. If he ever takes time out from these varied activities, he might be interested to read the conclusion of Law in Sport when it comes to FIFA's application of its own regulations to political gestures. It suggests that, 'FIFA is left to determine what it considers to be the actual nature of each [incident] ... and it is certainly a valid proposition to suggest that rules need to be capable of evolution to match the unpredictability of human behaviour.' Such flexibility may be all well and good, but, as the statement goes on to explain, 'The rules as they stand rely on consistency of application from FIFA, and in some instances that has appeared to present a challenge.'

A challenge indeed. The Arab Cup had been an apparently successful and, as far as one can judge from the evidence available, an enjoyable rehearsal for the authorities in Qatar. Whoever provides the copy for FIFA's website seems to have been given a brief to convey insipid blandness by dutifully reporting that 'Qatar proved outstanding hosts' and that 'the nation will be ready and waiting next year to welcome the teams that emerge from the ongoing qualifying competition for the FIFA World Cup Qatar™' in 2022. Nevertheless, even this exercise in dullness was an improvement on the efforts of those charged with maintaining the government's website, which was not updated about anything throughout the entire competition.

The Arab Cup had avoided controversy. The ubiquitous support for Palestine and the overt and unapologetic actions of the tournament's winners caused no friction in a country where pro-Palestinian sentiment runs with the grain of almost all popular opinion. FIFA had exercised flexibility: it was probably judicious to do so and there were no angry voices in its ear demanding anything else. The normally strident *Times of Israel* had nothing to say other than to briefly report on a low-key boycott of an insignificant post-tournament 'legends' game in Qatar by three Algerian players annoyed at the involvement of Israeli Avram Grant as manager of one of the teams. Nothing to see here; move on. No knees were taken, no rainbow laces worn, no undergarments so much as displayed the birth of a new-born or dedicated a goal to a departed parent. So far, so good. Particularly if you didn't really know your own rules and were prepared to turn a conveniently blind eye.

Just like the authorities hoped would happen when it came to whose hard work was making it all happen.

Chapter 7

If you build it ... don't think
that anyone will forget who
gave their lives for it

FOR AN EDUCATED man, I harbour far too many infantile prejudices when it comes to football. One of these is an inability to fully warm to anyone who has plied their trade with Aston Villa. As it happens, player and manager movement between Birmingham's two clubs (or three if you really insist on including the Albion) is far from rare. But memories tend to be shortened if any kind of success ensues. As it also turns out, the professed childhood allegiances of footballers need to be consumed with large amounts of salt. 'Yes, my grandad first brought me to St. Andrew's/Villa Park/The Hawthorns (delete as applicable) when I was just a nipper and the club's been in my blood since. Sometimes. All depending.' But I have to admit it: for all his connections with the neighbours,

I like Gareth Southgate – and I do so for a number of reasons.

Principal among these is the dignity and good sense that he brings to one of the most difficult jobs in the game, refusing to be ruffled into intemperate reaction to incidents or rising to the jibes of hacks eager for a cheap headline. From what one can gather, his qualities and approach have led to England players genuinely wishing to turn out for their country and openly buying into the notion of full collective responsibility. His extraordinary *Dear England* statement of June 2021 demonstrated a level of clarity, eloquence and empathy that, as so many in and beyond the game acknowledged, put the antics and flummery of elected politicians to shame. 'I know my voice carries weight,' he explained, 'not because of who I am but because of the position I hold … I have a responsibility to use my voice and so do the players.' His self-effacing acceptance that 'at home, I'm below the kids and the dog in the pecking order' would have raised a parental smile in plenty of households. His refusal to be cowed by those who opposed taking the knee, and who began to look more out of touch with every passing day, was particularly admirable.

With San Marino duly despatched and England's qualification for Qatar fully confirmed, Southgate again demonstrated his willingness to look at football's place in the wider world and his readiness to show his enduring sense of responsibility. His team 'would take the time to educate ourselves' about Qatar and 'if we feel that there are areas we can highlight and help, then we would do that'. All the same, he noted, 'we as a nation do a lot of business' with the hosts and this would mean stepping into a situation he recognised as 'highly complex'.

In 2010, immediate reaction from the world's press to Qatar's successful bid made enlightening reading. In the US, where there had been a strong feeling that their own bid had genuine weight, the outraged *Seattle Times* railed against 'dirty oil money' and asked whether 'the FIFA cartel [has] seriously lost its soul'. This fury was balanced by the more temperate *Kansas City Star* which asserted that 'bringing the World Cup to new places is the right thing to do' and reminded its readers that the 1994 award to the US was met with 'quite an outcry'. In Australia, another nation whose bid had failed, the *Brisbane Times* lamented an 'abject failure and embarrassment' at losing out to 'a tiny emirate of few people, little sporting pedigree … a nation in name but a city-state in practice'.

Europe's tabloids enjoyed the opportunity to air their usual nationalist predispositions. 'FIFA sold the 2022 World Cup to the sheiks,' spluttered Germany's *Das Bild*, dubbing the decision 'Qatarstrophe – this is how the word is spelt since yesterday'. Italy's *Gazzetta Dello Sport* expressed astonishment at Russia and Qatar being chosen when 'they had the worst dossiers'. Spain's *Marca* ruefully pondered how its own nations' organisational ability, already demonstrated at the Olympics and World Cups of football, basketball and swimming, had been overlooked. In the UK, *The Sun* decided, with wearying predictability, that it was all the fault of the BBC, whose 'cynical actions in broadcasting rehashed corruption allegations against FIFA on the eve of the vote' for the 2018 and 2022 competitions had undermined England's bid for the former and allowed open season for the real corruption that led to Qatar's success. Tellingly, it was left to newspapers from Indonesia and Singapore to offer alternative worldviews. The *Jakarta Globe* seemed to take quiet satisfaction at how western nations faced a 'struggle to come to terms' with the decision and the *Singapore Strait Times* happily announced, 'Qatar puts Middle-East football on the map'.

Amid all this initial reaction, the issue of workers' rights in Qatar – one of those areas, presumably, that Gareth and his players will wish to educate themselves – did not immediately surface. Such reticence did not last long. By June 2012, prior to any major World Cup infrastructure projects starting in Qatar, the organisation Human Rights Watch (HRW) adopted the sporting cliché and got its retaliation in first. In a report entitled *Building a Better World Cup*, it explained with shocking clarity the situation facing migrant workers in Qatar. It is unpleasant reading.

At the time of the report's publication, 1.2 million of 1.7 million residents of Qatar were migrant workers – 94 per cent of the population. Estimates of the further numbers required once the projects started in earnest indicated that anything up to another million people would be needed. The vast majority of migrant workers came from Pakistan, Bangladesh, India, Nepal and Sri Lanka and this remains the case. For most, acquiring work in Qatar necessitates paying a recruitment fee to an agency in the region of $3,500 and to access such funds means taking out high-interest loans. Reasons for undertaking such work usually arise from the desire to support families or, increasingly, to escape violence and conflict at home. Once in Qatar, having placed themselves in long-term debt and uprooted themselves from their communities and loved ones, much of what was promised turned out to have been at odds with the truth.

Squatting like a toad on the lives of all migrant workers is the *kafala* system. This is legislation that makes it mandatory for such workers to seek the sponsorship of a patron. Such patrons have the power to prevent them from changing jobs or even, in some cases, from leaving the country. This measure is particularly pernicious because once migrants arrive in the country, they face two major and unexpected problems, as their testimonies to HRW reveal. First, the actual jobs on offer bear little resemblance to what they had been led to expect and, second, wages are much reduced from what had been promised. At a rate of between $8 and $11 a day – sometimes as low as $6.75 – paying off recruitment fees becomes a distant and dismal prospect.

On top of these immediate obstacles come the conditions in which work is carried out, as well as the further impositions levied by employers. In its 2012 report, HRW reported on confidential interviews with migrant workers who consistently told of employers who made arbitrary, and largely illegal, deductions from wages to cover costs for visas, bedding, food and healthcare. Although Qatari legislation relating to labour camps stipulates that there should be no more than four people to a room, no use of bunk beds, easy access to drinking water and full air conditioning, such high standards were at variance with workers' experiences. HRW visited camps and found nowhere where there were fewer that eight people in a room, sometimes rising to 16. In all cases, all workers slept in bunk beds and in many there was no easy access to drinking water. Air conditioning was rarely fully operational.

Construction work, in which most of the migrants living in camps were engaged, was universally described as dangerous and unhealthy, often taking place in temperatures in excess of 40°C. In 2012, Qatar's Ministry of Labour called on the services of 150 inspectors for the 1.2 million migrants working there – roughly one inspector for 8,000 workers. Reports indicate that the ability to speak the language of workers was non-existent, which is almost irrelevant given that none of those interviewed ever recall coming across such official figures. Probably as a result of this ultra-light-touch scrutiny, government figures relating to accidents and death at work look just a touch optimistic. Conceding that 'workplace injuries are the third-highest cause of accidental deaths in Qatar', the Ministry of Labour explained that only six people had died in the construction industry in the three years to 2012 and that all of these had been as a result of falls. These figures provide a stark contrast to those provided by authorities in the home countries of migrant labourers. For example, in 2010, the Nepali embassy in Qatar reported that 191 Nepali workers had died in Qatar, 19 as a result of workplace accidents and a further 103 from cardiac arrest, despite the fact that the age profile of these fatalities was entirely inconsistent with such a cause of death.

By the time of HRW's report two years after the award to Qatar, and whether workers' rights had ever been on their radar or not, FIFA publicly woke up to the issue. Jerome Valcke, its secretary general, who had not yet joined the procession of the FIFA cabal to be dismissed for serial till-dipping, assured the footballing world that 'FIFA upholds the respect for human rights and the application of international norms of behaviour as a principle and part of all our activities'. What's more, he affirmed, FIFA would 'work jointly over the next few months to address labour issues with the Qatari authorities'. So, by the time Algeria jigged around with the Arab Cup at the fully completed Al Janoub Stadium in front of some 60,000 people, how many of the concerns of HRW and other campaigning organisations, including the International Trade Union Confederation, had been properly addressed?

In August 2021, Amnesty International published a 56-page report entitled *In the Prime of Their Lives*, which raised questions about the number of deaths of migrant workers in the previous decade. It conceded that from the low bar of 2010, progress has been made. It explains that 'since being awarded the 2022 FIFA World Cup in 2010, Qatar has made several significant positive reforms to its labour laws'. Legislation on its own, however, has not been enough to address a drastic situation. The report bemoans the fact that 'weak implementation and enforcement mean that progress on the ground has been slow and exploitation remains commonplace'. It draws the conclusion that 'many migrant workers remain at the mercy of unscrupulous employers who are allowed to commit abuses with impunity'.

Nowhere is this disregard for due process more evident than in the certification of deaths. Dr David Bailey, a leading pathologist and member of the World

Health Organisation, told Amnesty that a slapdash, catch-all approach to recording reasons for death was alarming in the extreme. 'There are phrases that should not be included on a death certificate without a further qualification explaining the underlying cause,' he explains. 'Essentially, everyone dies of respiratory or cardiac failure in the end and the phrases are meaningless without an explanation of the reason why.'

Government sources from Bangladesh, India, Pakistan and Nepal attribute around 70 per cent of deaths of their nationals in Qatar to 'natural causes'. When it comes to hard numbers of real people, official figures from Qatari authorities put non-Qatari deaths in the country between 2010 and 2019 as 15,201. While not all of these would have been migrant construction workers, the high percentage of such employees in the country strongly suggests that such people make up much of this figure. But while the Qatari authorities and its official bureaucrats try to cloak causes of death with bland labels, there is one factor that, as far as expert opinion is concerned, is indisputably to blame. Heat.

Before we look in detail at this single overriding factor, which was, of course, the immediate and obvious concern from the moment Blatter pulled out the winning envelope, it's worth seeing whether there have been any improvements since. It is impossible to know whether the initial Qatar bid, which envisaged the building of nine new stadia and three refurbishments, ever factored in concerns about the rest of the world scrutinising its antiquated view of workers' rights. Nevertheless, by the middle of the decade, some minor improvements, particularly in relation to working hours and enforced breaks, had been put into place. These, however, were far from universal. With outside, prying eyes focussed on the stadia – eventually whittled down to the eight to be used – any minor benefits that were granted were bestowed solely on those working on these developments. As campaigner and journalist Nicholas McGeehan explains, 'If you accept the humane logic that a worker building the road to a 2022 stadium deserves the same basic protection as a worker building the actual stadium, then don't accept an inhumane system that only grants protection to the tiny fraction of workers on the most visible projects.' A reminder, in other words, that the builders of football grounds aren't the only workers who need protection.

This discrepancy in terms of the protection afforded to those working beyond the stadia has played out in the cause of multiple deaths. A 2019 Qatari government report founds that such workers were at significantly higher risk of heat stroke than those working on specific World Cup projects. In the same year, the journal *Cardiology* found a correlation between heat and Nepali worker deaths in Qatar, concluding that 'as many as 200 of the 571 cardiovascular deaths (of Nepali workers) during 2009–17 could have been prevented' with effective heat protection measures.

For the avoidance of any doubt, when we talk about 'heat' in this context, we're dealing with conditions that go way beyond a scorcher on the summer-holiday beach. The internationally recognised standard for measuring heat stress is the Wet Bulb Globe Temperature (WBGT) which measures the combined effect of temperature, humidity, wind speed and solar radiation on the human body. At a WBGT of 29.3°C, an acclimatised worker can do moderately strenuous work for 45 minutes before requiring a 15-minute break. At 31.8°C, the ratio is reversed – 15 minutes' work for 45 minutes of rest. At a WBGT of 38°C, no work is possible. In September 2016 in Doha, the WBGT regularly reached 35°C; in one 72-hour period in the previous August, it remained constantly above 30.6°C.

Widespread testimony from workers to organisations like Amnesty and HRW consistently refer to inbuilt non-compliance to the work/rest formula on the part of employers and overseers. The link between scarcely explained deaths is clear. Professor Douglas Casa told HRW that such disregard for regulations relating to heat safety could only mean that 'there is a high probability that heat stroke played a role in many of the unexplained deaths or the deaths attributed to cardiac arrest'. By February 2021 a team of international journalists assembled by the

Guardian and drawing on a range of credible sources, put the actual number of deaths of migrant workers from the five major places from which such workers came – Nepal, Sri Lanka, Pakistan, Bangladesh and India – at 6,500. Put another way, these figures represent an average of 12 migrant workers from each of these countries dying every week since the award was made to Qatar.

To put that figure into some sort of context, it is worth pointing out that figures in the UK in the last decade, from both the Health and Safety Executive and the Office for National Statistics, reveal that construction remains the most dangerous occupation when it comes to workplace fatalities. In 2020/21, of 142 such workplace deaths, 39 were in the building trade – some 27 per cent of the total. It is a pattern that has been established since the 1990s and the numbers of such fatal accidents has remained stable since the start of the pandemic. Even given the extent of Qatar's ambitious building programme, which probably doesn't bear comparison with the nature and scale of infrastructure projects in the UK, an average death toll of around 650 a year in a workforce that is about one 13th the size is an alarming statistic.

What then of Southgate's undertaking to engage in education about such issues? In Amnesty's 2021 report, its UK CEO, Sacha Deshmukh, suggested, 'England players, staff and supporters can use their influence by keeping the issue of migrant worker rights in Qatar in the public eye. There is still an enormous amount to play for.' By the turn of 2022, there had been nothing forthcoming from the England team, although the disruption wrought by Covid on the English season's whirligig of crammed festive features could probably excuse any such reticence. Nevertheless, there was no sly evasion of the subject.

Even prior to the formality of the qualification confirmed by the San Marino game, there had been something of a reaction from Southgate's charges. Late in 2020, notwithstanding his brief international career, the Wolves captain, Conor Coady, had been included by the England manager in his leadership team. This select group is, by Southgate's admission, a somewhat fluid entity. 'In terms of the leadership group,' he explained, 'it ends up having to change every time we are together because we never, ever have a full squad to pick from.' Despite his relative inexperience, Coady, whose other media interviews had revealed an articulate, thoughtful and independent-minded young man, was probably a straightforward choice.

Citing their work with child poverty and support for the NHS, Coady pointed to the work of Marcus Rashford and Jordan Henderson, talking of how this was 'a fantastic part of this England group, the players make an incredible difference trying to use that platform to help'. When turning his attentions to concerns about labour and human rights in Qatar, he echoed the same reserve of his manager about considering it over time. 'At the minute,' he suggested in November 2021, 'it is tough to speak about it because it is not something we have had a real conversation about,' before going on to quell any suggestion that these were issues that would be put on the back-burner. 'We are not robots, we are humans, we are seeing things in the news that are going on every day,' Coady remarked, 'but we've always said to ourselves over the last year that the most important thing is to get to Qatar, and honestly speak about the situation when the time is right.'

Teams from other countries had already begun to make their moves. In March 2021, Norway's players lined up prior to kick-off in their qualifier against Gibraltar with t-shirts bearing the logo 'Human Rights On and Off the Pitch.' A few weeks later, Germany's players staged a similar protest before their game with Iceland. 'We have the World Cup coming up and there will be discussions about it,' said Germany midfielder Leon Goretzka. 'We have a large reach and we can use it to set an example for the values we want to stand for.'

Days before the draw that threw up the possibility of the return of the ghost of Belo Horizonte and a home nations clash in the dunes, England's squad was briefed about Qatar at their St George's Park headquarters. Reports suggest that there was no bored indifference in evidence. Jordan Henderson, acting as spokesperson for the squad, spoke of players now fully understanding situations that were 'shocking, disappointing and horrendous'. It was not their intention to turn blind eyes. 'As a team, we're just sort of digesting that, coming up with ideas of what we want to do going forward, because it's an opportunity to maybe shine a light on the issues and use our platforms to make changes for the better.' He spoke of the possibility of liaising with other teams to present a united form of opposition to, and recognition of, the abuses that had so shocked his colleagues. Henderson also acknowledged that his team-mates found themselves in something of a no-win situation. 'Whatever we decide to do will be criticised and will never be enough,' he explained, 'but we do it to try and make a difference.' Whatever they do decide, the reaction of these footballers is a world away from the appeasement of Hitler with Nazi salutes.

The title of this chapter borrows from the oft-misquoted line from director Phil Alden Robinson's 1989 modern film classic *Field of Dreams*. The central character, Ray Kinsella, played by Kevin Costner, is driven to pursue his dream of creating a baseball stadium by a voice in a cornfield insisting, 'If you build it, he will come.' Kinsella single-mindedly beats off adversity from all corners as he follows the dream and the stadium is completed. Ungraciously damned by some for its undisputed sentimental streak, *Field of Dreams* is, nevertheless, a testament to the kind of ridiculous dreaming and wild aspiration for which sport, as any rational human being will tell you, was invented. Sensible people are sucked into making preposterous commitments and hopes of glory are undiminished in the face of sound common sense (ask any fans of Derby or Bury). It is this faint and distant smell of success that brings children and their grandparents to scruffy non-league grounds on freezing afternoons, induced by the promise of burgers, grown-ups freely swearing and the possibility of chucking the ball back to a player. The eight glorious, space-age, streamlined stadia all so easily accessible from Doha will do well if they ever generate anything like that long-lasting love and loyalty. It would be good if they could, if only to properly honour the thousands whose indentured servitude had brought them into being.

Chapter 8

A beer in the sunshine? I'd chop your hand off for one. Joking, just joking

AT THE Euros in 2016, Welsh supporters manufactured one of the jewels in the crown of football songs. The sheer joy and cheekiness of the plea to stay where you were and keep drinking struck a chord with anyone who has gone to see their team play away in the hope that maybe, just maybe, this time the journey, the expense and the hassle of arranging time off from work will all be worthwhile. In terms of enjoyment and happiness, 'Don't Take Me Home' is an uplifting contrast to the weekly dirge from the grating playlist of away fans observing that your town's a shithole and they want to go home – which always prompts the query as to why you came here in the first place, then.

I know a bit about going away. One way and another, I've watched games at 67 of the current 92 grounds in the top four divisions and been to a fair few others that have since dropped to level five and below. What's more, I've seen my own team lose at 43 of them. I've seen us lose at 18 of the current 20 teams in the Premier League – and the only reason it isn't 20 is that I'm not counting losses at the old White Hart Lane, as I haven't been to the new stadium yet (and, as far as league fixtures are concerned, am not likely to do so in the foreseeable future) and neither have I been to wherever Brentford think is better than the splendid Griffin Park. I've witnessed a further 18 defeats at grounds in the current Championship and a smattering elsewhere. If I wanted to – and I promise you I don't – I could write another book about tedious, miserable journeys home I have endured over the decades.

In the other arena of my twin sporting obsessions, I have been fortunate to follow England's cricket teams abroad and have witnessed plenty of success. I will be able to meet my maker secure in the knowledge that I am one of a happy, select band of Englishmen to have witnessed an Ashes victory on Aussie turf. Going back to the 70s, I saw the occasional England game at Wembley and I've also been to international games as a neutral at World Cups and Euros in France and Germany. Very often on such occasions, it has been a pleasure to bump into other English football supporters, quite frequently recognisable by their (our) insistence on wearing (our) lower-league club shirts in bars, town squares and fan parks. On other occasions, it has been less agreeable to have been witness to churlish, grudging and snarling conduct from the worst sort of Ingerlund fan.

All of which is a backdrop to explaining that, for all my sporting travels, I have never watched England play football in another country. I should also explain that, although serious hooliganism has never been a part of my extensive football-watching life, I have seen it at very close hand on plenty of occasions. It's often ugly, sometimes farcical and the gap between reality and sensationalised folklore is a large one. Notwithstanding this degree of familiarity with the ways of the leery football supporter, readers should be in no doubt that had I been anywhere near the rucking between English and Russian followers in Marseilles in 2016, you'd have found me unashamedly behind the bins in the nearest back-alley.

It was the ill-feeling generated by this encounter, souped-up and enflamed as it had been by gleeful media in both countries, that partially accounted for an initial reluctance on the part of English supporters to follow their team to the 2018 World Cup in Russia. On top of this, even the most poorly informed football supporter would probably have been unnerved – no pun intended – by the poisoning of Sergei and Yulia Skripal in Salisbury in March 2018 and its effect on an alarming deterioration of relations between Russia and the UK. Beyond these considerations, as Kevin Miles, at the time the chair of the

Football Supporters' Federation and since appointed to the government's fan-led review of football, observed prior to the tournament, 'Things like the distances between venues, the cost of games ... and the fact that Russia is not a traditional holiday destination' all combined to make travelling there a relatively unattractive proposition for the everyday fan.

This early-tournament pessimism was echoed by pricing consultants Simon Kucher & Partners, whose initial estimates suggested that numbers of England supporters travelling to Russia would be down by some 15,000 on the 35,000 who had seen dear old Roy Hodgson's boys serve up the grim Brazilian appetiser to his final humiliation against Iceland two years later. Citing these low expectations, along with a price hike of 18 per cent to an average of £75 per game four years earlier, as well as concerns about safety and security, the consultants noted that only around 2,000 England supporters were in the crowd of 41,000 in Volgograd, where a late goal saw their team win their opening match against Tunisia.

Accounts suggest that, mercifully, those England supporters who did make it understood the enormous significance of the place they were visiting and conducted themselves with appropriate decency. Volgograd was formerly named Stalingrad, and, as such, at the centre of the World War Two campaign that, according to the massively authoritative historian Anthony Beevor, 'represented the most catastrophic defeat hitherto experienced in German history' and which, undoubtedly, definitively influenced the outcome of the entire war. Rather than mindlessly grunt out drivel from the shameful repertoire of England fans eager to invoke a conflict from which they had been spared by an accident of time and birth, many English visitors took time out to lay wreaths at the memorial of the thousands of Soviet dead. From the perspective some six weeks into Russia's invasion of Ukraine, such history is only too grimly alive.

One of those present at the memorial was 56-year-old Garford Beck from Hammersmith. He'd booked a £70 flight from Stansted to Istanbul, flown from there to Krasnodar for £56 and taken an overnight train to Volgograd for £12. He must have thought it was a bargain (of sorts) having 'spent thousands going to Brazil and we went out after two games'. Whether such barmy determination found its way into the calculations of Simon Kucher is unlikely, but I do know that it makes my grizzling about driving back from miserable defeat at Barnsley look a touch lame. Given developments since, there won't be many fans from anywhere who'll be able to tell tales of derring-do on the trail to Russia.

But if Garford's resolve and purpose is something, possibly, of an extreme case, when it comes to forging a pathway to football-watching overseas, he's by no means an exception. I've seen it enacted at both international and, believe it or not, very briefly at club level.

In 2011, following Birmingham City's unlikely League Cup win in February – tarnished immediately by relegation in May, of course – my club went on its own little European adventure. It involved excursions to Nacional in Madeira, Braga in Portugal, Maribor in Slovenia and a truly legendary night in Bruges. In all the urban myths that surrounded these unexpected brushes with football's romanticism, stories abounded of how fans had made their various ways to these destinations. This was particularly true of Maribor where, incidentally, there was more than one report of contented bar owners closing early to count their takings, having been drunk entirely dry by thirsty Brummies on a mission. With few direct flights to Slovenia, enterprising supporters took their chances on planes, trains and automobiles from Italy, Austria, Croatia and Hungary. Some had match tickets, plenty did not and practically all got into the games. The very idea that non-possession of this seemingly vital component of a football trip might be a deterrent to travel is utterly laughable.

When it came to the more accessible destination of Bruges, thousands of fans did exactly what I had done on my jaunts to France and Germany. They got together with a group of mates, hired a mini-bus, booked a few cheap and cheerful pit-stop hotels and set off on a jolly.

Now, nobody is suggesting that this cavalier attitude makes a bunch of people going to football the equivalent of Shackleton surveying the icy wastes and stepping out reliant only on wit, bravery and tins of corned beef. But it highlights stark contrasts about being a football supporter. Beyond official travel groups and members of accredited supporters' clubs with allocated blocks of tickets, will Qatar accommodate the spirit of Garford Beck? And if, as happened in Russia, England's progress prompts people to look for very last-minute packages, as some 10,000 of them did for the 2018 semi-final against Croatia in Moscow, just how welcoming will the hosts be?

In early 2022, at the risk of being bombarded over the coming weeks with unsolicited emails from Qatar Airways and a few other providers, I tapped in some fictitious travel plans. A return flight that would have given me ten days at the group stages of the tournament came in at around £800 from a range of airlines. Hotels were a different story: there were none available. All, no doubt, were already earmarked for packages that were in place or would be pretty soon. So what if I were to book such a package?

The two obvious places to start were the websites of Sportsworld, the official FA travel partner for the Qatar tournament and, after that, that of FIFA. The former could only promise that an initial ten-night package would soon be on offer, covering all of England's group matches with the temptation of individual short stays 'should England continue their fine form'. Their counterparts over at FIFA, whose officials had probably already collared the penthouses, were quicker off the mark. Because if there's one thing we know about the overlords of world football it's this: it's money that does the talking and nobody needs any reminding of that in the house that Sepp built.

'Hospitality' packages for group games began at $950, rising to $3,050. For the avoidance of doubt, that's just for the game itself. However, who could argue that this wasn't a bargain, given that your $950 secured 'temporary hospitality space located in the festive hospitality village within the stadium security perimeter' – which, one can only assume, means a decent seat. There was plenty else on offer. As well as soft drinks, wine and beer, the availability of which we will consider more fully in due course, there was the promise of 'trendy, global street-food-style dining for people on the move' – and all of this made particularly convenient by the provision of free parking. Well, there you go. A couple of pints (probably in a plastic glass), a hot dog, or even a samosa, a decent seat and a quick getaway from the carpark – it's the match-goer's dream.

The hotels on offer in FIFA's packages started from $337 per night and flights from an unspecified starting point from $475. Put that together with the $950 for your group game and a quick cheapskate spree out to the desert as an early bird, just to say you'd been, would rattle up a bill of some $1,700. Perhaps more realistically, the Travel Weekly website calculated that these early packages, albeit without specifying the number of games included, would work out at about £2,815, or $3,800.

None of which should come as any surprise. Sports Mega Events of all sorts always look to hoover up the rich pickings of the hospitality market at the earliest opportunity. On the release of these earlier packages, the chief executive of Qatar Airways Group, Akbar Al Baker, talked of facilitating 'a fulfilling experience' allowing fans to enjoy 'a seamless journey' that will be entirely 'hassle-free'. I think we can confidently assume that the intended audience for these firm assurances was not a group of half-organised drinking buddies piling into a transit with a few ragged holdalls and an assortment of boxed-up beers from Morrisons.

Football in the UK has a symbiotic relationship with beer. This is not, however, a purely national trait. In the spirit of academic inquiry, I undertook a brief trawl of some serious work that has been conducted on the relationship between beer and supporters in places ranging from Mexico to Australia. In a definitive study of 2013, academic Susan Dun of Northwestern University in Doha reached the nuanced and sophisticated conclusion that 'alcohol and football are like two peas in a pod for most football fans'. I can only hope she received a significant grant for this illuminating research. To be fairer to her, however, her work was an early attempt to consider how to understand the nature of Qatar's history and culture and the potential problems of accommodating 'the deeply ingrained beliefs and practices that surround the use of public space and exposure to what are believed to be toxic substances, such as alcohol'.

Dun's work was a serious and thorough attempt to cast some light on a complex situation. The immediate reaction of others was more one-dimensional. The organisation The Drinks Business was quick off the mark in 2014 in assessing the potential dent in profits from what would normally be a red-letter day on its global calendar. Its report in 2014 suggested that 'football fans hoping to enjoy a pint over a match may be left disappointed, along with the world's big brewers who more often than not benefit from a boost in sales thanks to such world sporting events'. An interview with sports minister Salah bin Ghanem bin Nasser al-Ali had not been particularly revealing. 'As we bid for 2022, we will respect all the rules and regulations by FIFA,' he explained to the nervous booze merchants. 'We can study this and minimize the impact on our people and tradition [but] I think we can be creative, finding solutions for all of this.'

In the meantime, still smarting, no doubt, about the combined treacheries of the BBC, FIFA magnates and those cheating foreigner types, *The Sun* in 2019 screeched out its prediction that 'footie fans' would 'vow to shun Qatar's 2022 World Cup as they run out of beer'. Now I'm sure the investigative prowess of Britain's best-selling tabloid is entirely unimpeachable, but quotes from 'an expat pilot, 30' bemoaning the fact 'if this isn't sorted, they'll be hosting the most miserable World Cup ever' – a judgement delivered some three years prior to kick-off – doesn't exactly put scribblers Nick Parker and Adam Bennett up there with Woodward and Bernstein. 'It's a national shortage,' revealed an anonymous barman from the W Hotel. 'If only we had some time to sort it out.' Of course I made that last bit up.

The Sun had chosen to run its story at just about the same time that the FIFA Club World Cup in Qatar was playing out to the delight of Liverpool's global audience, if not to many people in the actual stadia. It was the first opportunity for Qatar's authorities to try out the notion of 'wet fan zones' – and, yes, I'd definitely have called it something different too. These appear to have been moderately patronised, principally by members of the expat community, with prices at a perfectly reasonable £5 per pint. Berthold Trenkel, COO at Qatar Tourism, expressed satisfaction with the experiment but remained firmly reserved about the more contentious notion of drinking outside such areas. 'There will be some [places] where they will make it [alcohol] available and some where they won't,' he explained, before reminding potential visitors that 'public drunkenness and drinking alcohol in public places are not permitted'.

Mr Trenkel wouldn't be drawn on whether one of those places would be the tent camps, three of them, that were being planned by November 2021. Accommodating between 1,000 to 3,000 people – 'I don't yet have the final numbers' – these would be located on the outskirts of Doha and out in the wider desert. Those fans who managed to acquire a place could allay their fears about being roasted under their own canvas. Although daytime temperatures in December average around 25°C, Trenkel informed journalists that 'at night [it] is going to be 16°C to 17°C … you don't need AC – this is the time of year where I save electricity and turn it off'. Trenkel would not be drawn on whether the campsites would be potential venues for a civilised beer together under the desert moon.

In selected hotels and clubs in the city, alcohol, often overpriced because of this exclusivity, has always been available. However, with only 30,000 hotel rooms in a city expecting some 1.2 million visitors, only a small percentage of them would be able to enjoy this costly privilege. Even if 3,000 further fans were to be snuggling down in the chill of the tented evening, that still left plenty of rooms to find. Step forward the French hotel company Accor. In October 2021 the company signed a deal with the Qatari National Tourism Authority, with the full backing of the wider government, to manage some 60,000 existing residential villas and apartments in the country. The package, the value of which was not made public, ensured that Accor would be responsible for a wrap-around service from initial letting to housekeeping.

Unsurprisingly, the company's CEO, Sébastien Bazin, was delighted with this coup. In true statement-bank corporate-speak, he spilled out the usual clichés about being 'thrilled to have been selected to manage and provide services to Qatar's exciting real estate portfolio … excitement for the coming year … welcoming visitors … comfortable and memorable stay in the country'. He was probably relieved to see Accor in a more approving light than when it hit the headlines some two years earlier. In March 2019, the company had been forced to issue a fulsome apology after it emerged that it had operated a de facto apartheid system when allocating rooms and services to indigenous people at its Ibis Styles Hotel in Alice Springs, Australia.

Having overseen an arrangement whereby indigenous people were allocated inferior rooms, this was compounded by the level of service offered. An email provided by a whistleblower reminded staff that 'we are now only putting hospital linen into rooms 85 to 90 … these rooms are to be referred to as community rooms and we will try to limit them to just that, those coming from the communities [a local term for aboriginals from outside the town]'. By the end of the year, investors were beginning to express concern about the breadth and efficiency of the company's operations. This, along with the pandemic, resulted in revenues falling 60 per cent to €1.6bn in the 12 months that followed. The acquisition of the Qatar contract would have gone some way to calming any nerves and to making Bazin more relaxed about his prediction of 'a recovery to pre-2020 levels'.

One more accommodation contingency was planned on top of the hotel packages, Accor's apartments and the primus stoves and crusty sleeping bags – although one imagines the latter would be more about glamping than 'Ging Gang Goolie' and gin round the campfire. By the start of 2022, two huge cruise ships had been commissioned from the Swiss company MSC. With some 4,000 cabins and capacity for around 6,000 people, the vessels are fully equipped with spas, swimming pools and, of course, bars. What's more, according to the vice-chair of the Supreme Committee for Delivery and Legacy, Fatima Fakhro, this would be an eco-friendly innovation, producing the absolute minimum in terms of gas emissions and equipped with the latest technology to treat waste and water. Notwithstanding the UKs tabloids' elation about booze-cruises and revelry – 'a celebrity-filled extravaganza with party ships drafted in to keep the booze flowing,' yelped the *Mirror* – Qatari authorities remained more cautious. It was down to Berthold Trenkel to dampen expectations, reminding visitors that while Qatar is a hospitable place 'alcohol is not part of local culture'.

All of which begs the inevitable question: to what extent might these laws about alcohol be infringed and, crucially, how energetic will Qatari authorities be when it comes to enforcing them? As far as who will be actually setting off for Qatar, writing as winter fades in England some eight months before kick-off, it remains difficult to imagine that the lads-in-a-van constituency will be in the ascendancy. The strong likelihood remains that the majority of visitors will be from the more genteel, corporate-tolerant end of the football-supporting world. I'd be tempted to say 'think Arsenal at the Emirates' but that would be something of a disservice to the number of dyed-in-the-wool stalwarts who steadfastly support their team – now dubbed, apparently, legacy supporters. Maybe Liverpool fans from Singapore? Soccer followers from Miami? Anyway, you get the point. Our best guess has to be that for the majority shelling out the thousands to get there and stay for a few days, a lager-fuelled conga down the Corniche is probably not on the must-do list. Covid travel restrictions could yet put a few fireworks under the entire bonfire.

So, at the risk of making a prediction which will be made to look absurd with the passing of time, things should probably remain on the respectable side of matchday partying. Certainly, with the exceptions of the pockets of behaviour referred to earlier, that has been my experience of football tournaments abroad – a tolerant but boisterous atmosphere, with alcohol, like it or not (and I do) firmly at the centre. Still, what if? What if things go awry? What if merriment turns sour? What happens then?

Most of us carry a vague notion of the draconian punishments meted out in Arab countries. These are gleaned from occasional media stories, half-heard news reports, tales, anecdotes and episodes vaguely remembered. The murder of journalist Jamal Khashoggi, the explicit details of which became open knowledge, seemed confirmation of this inclination towards, and acceptance of, brutal actions in this part of the world. What is the truth behind these impressions that spring so easily to mind?

The first thing to establish is that talk of the 'Middle East' when addressing this issue isn't helpful: different countries in the region conduct themselves in a variety of ways when it comes to how offenders are punished. At the most extreme end of the scale is the use of capital punishment – although, to forgo accusations of scaremongering, there is no suggestion that a drunken wee down the alley of a posh hotel would merit the ultimate sanction. An Amnesty report in 2020 identified four countries in the region – Iran, Egypt, Iraq and

Saudi Arabia – as responsible for 88 per cent of global executions in 2020. These figures are given against the significant caveat that it is suspected that China executes people in hundreds, possibly thousands, each year, but such numbers remain a state secret. The same goes for North Korea and Vietnam. The available data reveals 437 executions in the Middle East in 2020, down from 579 in 2019 and due largely to a diminution of such cases in Saudi Arabia – that is, prior to its killing spree in March 2022, just prior to hosting the Grand Prix. As far as Qatar is concerned, the report noted with disappointment that the country had carried out its first execution for 20 years in 2020 when a Nepali was killed by firing squad having been found guilty of murder.

But, to repeat the point, even the most pessimistic, or ill-informed, supporter would not reckon on death row for a night on the beer. As awful as executions and the reporting around them might be, it is the spectre of other corporal punishments – floggings, amputations – that haunt popular imagination. Saudi Arabia is, perhaps, seen as the most enthusiastic purveyor of such practices, although figures suggest that it has some way to go to catch up with the judiciary across the Gulf in Iran. However, by April 2020, Saudi's rulers decreed that floggings would no longer be an acceptable punishment in the kingdom. 'This reform is a momentous step forward in Saudi Arabia's human rights agenda, and merely one of many recent reforms in the kingdom,' said Awwad Alawwad, the president of the state-backed Human Rights Commission. Significantly, there was no word on capital punishment or amputations and an unremarkable silence on state-sanctioned dismemberment of journalists in foreign embassies.

Qatari law still has flogging as part of its repertoire of penalties, although reputable sources seem to indicate that its use is relatively rare, especially in comparison to its Saudi neighbours. While alcohol consumption, adultery and apostasy are punishable by flogging, this applies only to Muslims. The secular law, which would be in use for travelling supporters, would look to financial penalties, which are easily the most favoured sanction in the entire Qatari legal system. Speaking in 2016, Dr Najeeb al-Nuaimi, Qatar's former minister of justice, was keen to point out this distinction, along with the fact that amputations for stealing were a thing of the past, recognising that such crimes often stemmed from necessity or deprivation. Oh, and even when it came to flogging, culprits kept their clothes on and measures were in place – often a book under the armpit – to prevent the lashes being administered too energetically. Well, there's progress for you.

In short, therefore, the sensible punter who wants a drink in the matchday sun will probably be OK. The proximity of the various stadia and the housing of the entire event around one city – making it closer to the staging of an Olympics than a traditional World Cup – might yet set a challenge in terms of supporter clashes and public order. There could yet be an issue of how many fans will spend non-matchdays – a glimpse at the Visit Qatar website provides, well, thin-ish fare. In short, it's going to be different.

And that's the point: it's not what 'we' expect ... and that, of course, begs the major question about who 'we' are and who we think we are. I think the answer to that is challenging but simple – and forgive me if I start from a parochial point of view.

In my narrow universe, football lives in a world where I played and loved the game at a mud-splattered level and with that love living on as I bump a ball around with my grandkids in the garden. It exists in a logic-defying loyalty to the team I've supported for 60 years and a dogged insistence in trudging along to watch them in the very embodiment of the triumph of hope over experience. It exists in the cold and the rain and in pubs and steamy cafes. Every other summer it exists in watching England in the tournament sunshine and in sneering, ever so quietly, at those temporary converts to the game who are forced to fleetingly experience the dashed expectations that are the very essence of my footballing self. It exists – and here I'm being nakedly and shamefacedly truthful – in being mildly surprised to see people from China,

Japan and New Zealand being so good at the game. The spirit of how we saw the '66 Koreans lives on.

Beyond the press and media surprise at Qatar's successful bid, I lost count of the number of times I heard comments expressing outrage at the competition going to a country 'with no footballing tradition'. The plain fact is that such notions of tradition are lazy, sentimental and deeply conservative. The most inattentive reader will have picked up my lack of respect for FIFA and its overall conduct, but in terms of taking its premium competition around the globe, it has been successful. Will its success grow the game in Qatar? Will we see lobbying for Al Sadd SC (current Qatar Stars League champions, in case you're wondering) to enter the bloated Champions League? Possibly not, but we might well see Qatari interest in acquiring more of Europe's top clubs. And if we do, where would be the significant protest against that happening? If anyone thinks Qatar, with or without a beer, isn't part of a new football tradition, then they need to sharpen up. In terms of immediate success on the field, it may not be a member of a new world order, but its influence on who might be first up on *Match of the Day* – and the growing difference in quality between that team and yours – could well have its roots in Doha and its environs.

And who knows if football ever will come home or not. But even if it does, we could do ourselves a favour and remember that not everyone thinks the UK and Europe still sit in the middle of everyone's map of the world ... and now we're off to see one of those parts of the globe ...

Chapter 9

Down in Africa where parts of the map were once red, Doha would have been playing close attention

IAN WRIGHT was a fantastic footballer. A career total of 324 goals in 626 games across all competitions – better than one every two games – speaks for itself. His 185 for Arsenal, topped only by Thierry Henry, endowed him with justifiable legendary status. Even before his illustrious media career, it was plain to anyone watching that he was an awkward so-and-so. His former team-mate Lee Dixon recalls how 'Wrighty was the most horrible, annoying player you could ever play against … he just used to really wind everyone up'. Recalling an encounter in which Wright threw an ineffectual right hook at Steve Bruce in the tunnel at Old Trafford – and much as I harbour a soft spot for Brucey, I'll go along with the quip that if the punch had landed, it'd have improved his looks – Dixon fondly remembers how, if there was any trouble going, 'Wrighty would be in the thick of it'. Like I say, none of that comes as any sort of surprise to anyone who'd witnessed the unadulterated energy he brought to his game.

He has since brought that same level of commitment to his commentary about football and the wider issues associated with it. His unvarnished studio style leaves viewers and listeners in no doubt about where he stands on a range of issues. Nowhere is this more evident than in his unapologetic calling out of racism both within and beyond the game. His reward for his outspokenness is a daily diet of racist social-media trash, all of which appears to make him even more determined to speak out. Along with his willingness to use his own fractured life as a means of helping others, Wright's public profile is hugely impressive.

Which all means that when he spoke out at the end of December 2021 about perceptions of the forthcoming Africa Cup of Nations (AFCON), his was a voice that merited our attention. Wright was adamant that the attitude of the media and some in the game was 'disrespectful' and 'tinged with racism' when it came to this major competition. His criticisms were focussed on several telling issues. The first of these was the notion that players themselves might not be inclined to answer the call to play for their country. 'Imagine that was an

England player representing the Three Lions,' he told the BBC. 'Can you imagine the furore?'

Second, when it came to staging the tournament in Cameroon and the potential dangers arising from Covid and travel, he was justifiably bemused. The Euros had recently been played across ten countries in Europe. A quick number crunch reveals that concerns about using Cameroon as a venue certainly didn't stem from any close statistical analysis. With an annual per capita share of Gross Domestic Product (GDP) of just under $4,000 per person and sitting in 97th place in the global GDP rankings, Cameroon's population of some 26 million gets by on one tenth of the income enjoyed by people in the UK. The World Bank estimates that 24 per cent of this population lives in absolute poverty. At the start of the AFCON, Cameroon had registered just over 109,000 deaths from Covid – around one in 245 of the population. The figure in the UK, sixth in the global rankings, was about one death in 453 – which represents no great shakes given such overwhelming advantages.

Wright's concerns were echoed by a formidable ally. Given his predisposition to a touch of on-field provocation, it must have given the striker some considerable confidence to glance over his shoulder to see the imperious figure of Patrick Vieira flaring his cold, hard stare at prospective combatants. Vieira has, perhaps, surprised many with his successful venture into management, although one imagines it would be a brave, or stupid, player who would cross this particular gaffer – not that this reputational advantage ever helped Roy Keane make much of an impact in his managerial adventures. Crystal Palace's Vieira would find himself without Cheikhou Kouyate, Wilfried Zaha and Jordan Ayew, but he was adamant that AFCON should be treated with due respect. Emphasising that he viewed the competition as important as the Euros, Vieira, whose mantelpiece displays winners' medals from both that tournament and the World Cup, talked of how he understood 'the passion and the importance to players to go and represent their country, so I will never stop any player going to play the Africa Cup of Nations'.

The outspokenness of these two revered players from the English league's recent past underlined a truth that many of football's professional chatterers failed to understand: there is no longer any uncontested 'ownership' of the beautiful game. There may be tradition and history aplenty in the leagues that were first established around the globe in the last century and a half, but however deeply entrenched the game may be in the hearts and minds of those of us from those geographical regions, the idea that it 'belongs' anywhere no longer bears sensible scrutiny.

But AFCON did manage to demonstrate one of football's most enduring and attractive truths: it retains the capacity to produce results that defy any logic, form or expectation. The group stages furnished us with two delicious instances. Algeria came to the tournament as African champions and fresh from their success in the Arab Cup. They were also on a run of 34 matches unbeaten, with the strong possibility that they could challenge Italy's record of 37, which had come to end with defeat by Spain in October 2021. Held to a goalless draw in their opening game with Sierra Leone, Algeria then lost to a single goal from full-back Esteban Obiang against Equatorial Guinea, 85 places below them in FIFA rankings.

The magnitude of this result, bringing Algeria's unbeaten run to an end and jeopardising their continuing participation, merited some media coverage in the UK. But just to emphasise football's persistently parochial nature, the headline on Manchester City's official website took some beating. 'Mahrez's Algeria dealt surprise AFCON defeat,' it screeched, above a photo of the player bearing an anguished look ... and wearing his Man City shirt. The brief match report that follows is dedicated almost entirely to the contribution of 'our no. 26' and finishes with the information that despite the defeat, Algeria 'can still qualify for the knockout stages should they beat the Ivory Coast by two goals or more in their final group match this Thursday'. It doesn't go quite as far as to say 'so perhaps our no. 26 might soon get back to playing proper football', but there must have been wry smiles of relief when, four days later, Algeria were completely rolled over by Cote D'Ivoire, meaning Riyad could, indeed, jet back to do his day job.

His blushes, and those of his mates, were spared by an even greater upset two days later in the northern port city of Garoua. In 2010, Ghana – the Black Stars – had reached the last eight of the World Cup in South Africa, the only team outside Europe or South America to do so. They were also four-time winners of AFCON, albeit with their last success coming in 1982. Sitting in 52nd place in FIFA's rankings, they could count themselves an established, if middling, force in world football. They'd started the competition badly with defeat against Morocco and then managed a draw against Gabon. All of which meant that they came into their final group game needing a victory to give them any chance of qualifying – an outcome that should have been a formality against the Comoros (I promised they'd reappear). Sitting 132nd in the rankings, hailing from a group of islands in the Indian Ocean east of Malawi and drawing from a population of around a million, their team consisted mainly of players from France's lower leagues.

It will be a game that Ghana's goalkeeper will be happy to erase from his memory. Beaten by two shots, one in the opening minutes and the other on the hour, Swindon Town's Joe Wollacott will look at the footage and consider that he really should have done better with both. By the time the second went in, putting Comoros two up, he was playing in a team reduced to ten men. Ghana's captain, the well-travelled Andre Ayew, could consider himself very unlucky to have been the victim of a VAR-assisted red card following a challenge on Wollacott's opposite number. Ghana, however, managed to draw level, scoring twice in ten minutes following some clownish defending at two successive corners. But true order, far from being restored, was disrupted again as Comoros fashioned a good goal – this time free of keeper blame – with 12 minutes to go and then saw the game through to victory.

Like Riyad up in the sunny uplands of the Prem, it left Joe free to go back and ply his trade with his regular employers at the County Ground. Whether they thought his exertions in Africa had taken their toll, or if it was just a case of him not being worth a place (he'd put in 12 appearances before setting off for Cameroon), he found himself on the bench for the following Saturday's 1-1 draw at home to Bristol Rovers. Whatever the reason, I'm going to offer him a scrap of consolation.

He should probably have done better with the goals at Garoua, but I'll say with some confidence that however his season and career progress, I guarantee he will not put in a worse goalkeeping performance than the one I witnessed at his home ground on a chilly February day in 2000. In 1995, the football manager known as Barry Fry acquired the services of non-league Dutch keeper Bart Griemink, who put in 20 nerve-jangling performances at Birmingham City. This launched him on a decent enough career around the lower leagues including a spell at Swindon where, on that February day, he contrived, to our unbridled hilarity, to chuck in three of the goals in his team's 4-1 defeat at the hands of those that brought him to English football. And he certainly never had any international caps to brighten his 300-game career, Joe.

Whether or not the absence of other players from the English leagues detrimentally affected the performances of their clubs was difficult to assess. The start of the year saw a hotch-potch of cancellations because of Covid issues mixed with injuries and suspensions, all of which imposed a disjointed feel to events. Despite its relative availability on Sky, as well as conveniently timed kick-offs, AFCON still failed to cut through the clatter of the football showcase. What was also clear was the fact that crowds weren't flooding into Cameroon's stadia either. This was not, however, a sign of lack of interest.

The Confederation of African Football had decided prior to the tournament that ground capacity should be limited to 80 per cent for games involving Cameroon and 60 per cent for others. Fans also had to provide a negative PCR test as well as a vaccination certificate to enter stadia. In a country where two per cent of the population was estimated to have been vaccinated prior to the first game, this proved to be something of an obstacle. Official attendance figures were unobtainable from any sources during the competition, but the swathes of empty seats visible from TV footage told a clear story. Even the intervention of Africa's second-longest-ruling president, Paul Biya, failed to make an impact. On 15 January he announced that for the remainder of the competition, workdays would finish at 2pm and all school classes and university lectures at 1pm so that people could watch matches in the stadia. There were credible rumours of free tickets and transport circulating in the capital, Yaoundé.

But a combination of factors still kept people away. Tickets priced between $5 and $34 might not have been too far out of the range of the average Cameroonian salary of around $1,500 per month, but the added impediment of the Covid pass proved a step too far for some. And then there was the extra attraction of a cheap and very cheerful alternative – the many fan parks established on the outskirts of some cities. 'Here, you just need some cash for drinks, and you sit and enjoy the match,' Yaoundé resident Paul told Al Jazeera while watching Cameroon grind out a 1-1 draw against Cape Verde. 'To go to the stadium, you need a match ticket, a vaccination card and a negative PCR test. That's too much for me.' He was backed up by another local, Odette Abega, who turned up at the fan zone with her three children and told the TV station that the vibes and atmosphere were similar to that inside the stadium. 'There's a large screen here. I laugh and enjoy the games here without anybody asking for a Covid test or vaccination card. We Cameroonians love football, and we have devised a means to watch the games outside the stadium.'

There is no way of knowing whether Paul or Odette changed their minds and tried to attend the game between the host nation and Comoros on 24 January. Let's hope they didn't. As crowds made their way through the various checkpoints before arriving at turnstiles at the Olembe Stadium, they were met with obstructions and barriers before the main entrance. In the crush that ensued, at least eight people were killed and some 40 seriously injured.

In a straight lift from the David Duckenfield playbook of victim blaming, Cameroon's government had little immediate doubt as to where the blame lay. 'While welcoming the enthusiasm shown by the Cameroonian populations since the start of the tournament,' their press release read, 'the Government calls once again for the sense of responsibility, discipline and civic-mindedness for the total success of this great sporting celebration.' And lest any of us should smugly content that it could never happen in our orderly post-Hillsborough world, the report of Baroness Casey into the riot at Wembley prior to the Euro final the previous July was clear that it was only a matter of luck that there had been no fatalities.

Would Qatar's organisers have been looking on ready to learn any lessons? There may well have been significant numbers of migrant workers ready to make the trip to stadia in and around Doha for the Arab Cup, but their numbers would not have approached the estimated tens of thousands who turned up at the Olembe Stadium. The notion that there might be free tickets knocking about to be picked up on the off-chance in Doha is not one that is likely to be factored into their thinking. That is, of course, if they were paying any sort of attention anyway. It may not have been because of racist disrespect, but the eyes of the world tended to be elsewhere while AFCON played out to its conclusion. Putin's troops massed on Ukraine's borders; to the west of Cameroon in Burkina Faso, a military coup went practically unnoticed and at home we were treated to daily stories of jolly times and high jinks in the chambers of the prime minister. And, just because it was more than six weeks since they'd last done so, Watford sacked their manager.

Joe Wollacott wasn't the only lower-league player to experience top international competition at AFCON. Gambia, knocked out by the hosts in the quarter-finals, called on the services of two players from the same division as Swindon. Salford's Ibou Touray and Forest Green Rovers' Ebou Adams. They were among the 18 players from the EFL who travelled, along with 34 from the Premier League. From the top flight, only Leeds, Norwich, Tottenham and Newcastle were not called upon to provide players. In case the Saudi-acquired Geordies felt they were missing out, the club decided that some bonding in the warm weather of the land of their patrons was just the thing to do to launch their campaign to avoid relegation. 'It's a football decision,' explained Newcastle manager Eddie Howe. 'We're doing it for the benefit of the players in our fight to stay in the division and that's my only thought. The facilities and everything around the trip are going to be first-class and the players will be very well looked after.'

Howe always appears to the outside observer as intelligent, well-informed and thoughtful. His appetite for knowledge about the game is legendary. He spent the vacant months between jobs before accepting the Newcastle post assiduously chasing knowledge and expertise throughout the footballing world. He is renowned as a complete football obsessive, spending hours addressing detail and data as an integral part of his job brief. None of which casts him as either nerdy or aloof when speaking in front of cameras, where he comes across as measured and temperate in his comments. But on one issue, this smart, personable young man remains resolutely tight-lipped. When it comes to expressing an opinion about the human rights record of the regime from which his employers hail – and of which, let's not beat about the bush, they are a part – he will utter not a word. He could do with having a word with Jordan Henderson about moral leadership.

In many ways, of course, Howe's outlook is entirely unsurprising. Biting the hand that feeds you is never a good look. But when pressed on whether he would shake the hand of Mohammed bin Salman, recognised almost universally as the leader under whose watch shocking abuse takes place, Howe deflected the question with talk of 'no distractions' and the benefits of training in 'a different environment'. Gareth Southgate, who had made the firm undertaking to educate himself and his players about human rights abuses in neighbouring Qatar, will have looked on with interest – although it is fair and proper to point out that managing a club operating under direct sponsorship is very different from oversight of a national team. However, if nothing else, Gareth would have possibly breathed a sigh of relief that the bar had been set so low. It's also worth observing that initial protests and banners decrying Newcastle's owners – both at St James' Park and elsewhere – seem to have been worthy but short-lived. The mercurial nature of such protest was probably also greeted with satisfaction in the boardrooms of Doha.

As the Toon players did their shuttle-runs in the sun and hatched their plans to avoid the drop, the Saudi Public

Investment Fund (PIF), the body that had, to all intents and purposes, laundered the state's bid for their club, dipped its toe a little further into the sportswashing water.

With the sideshow of golf's Saudi International playing out in Jeddah, the PIF had commandeered the services of one of the game's genuine legends, Greg Norman, to be the front man for a proposed alternative tour to be staggeringly financed by the Saudi state. This was to be golf's version of football's (temporarily) failed Super League. 'This is only the beginning,' proclaimed Norman, going on to point out that top players were independent contractors who 'can play where they want'. Initial rumours of appearance fees running to tens of millions for such players immediately began circulating. *Guardian* journalist Ewan Murray managed to speak to one, who insisted on anonymity. When asked if his actions might not play well against a public perception that sportsmen of his standing already enjoy sufficient wealth, his response was that nobody would choose to downscale their life if there was an alternative on offer. There must have been plenty of agents and heads of Saudi corporations nodding sagely at such obvious common sense ... and, no doubt, compiling their lists of who to take to lunch when the World Cup arrived next door.

Meanwhile, AFCON continued to play out, punctuated by some terrific finishing, slapstick defending and a series of interchanges between referees and VAR officials that were as baffling as they were consistently comic. One person who would have been grateful to these matches for diverting people's attention was FIFA President Gianni Infantino – the man who, although having partially fulfilled his brief to rid his organisation of the stench of Blatter, proved himself to be no stranger to a private jet and a plump expenses claim.

In an almost surreal moment, while extolling the advantages of holding a World Cup every two years, he told a parliamentary assembly at the Council of Europe, 'We need to find ways to include the whole world to give hope to Africans so that they don't need to cross the Mediterranean in order to find maybe a better life but, more probably, death in the sea.' Perhaps he was attempting to impress this prestigious political body with his grasp of affairs beyond football. Whatever the reason for this bizarre observation, he had the good sense to retract it almost immediately, but for a man on an annual salary of $1.5m – or so we think, because, surprisingly, FIFA's accounts lack transparency on the matter – it was one of a long line of gaffes from men who, to coin a current footballing cliché, really should be better than that.

The latter stages of AFCON provided little football of any genuine quality and few matches of high drama – always accepting that we exclude penalty shoot-outs from that analysis. Mo Salah's Egypt – yes, of course it was his – were afforded the opportunity to display some real expertise in this aspect of the game. After a goalless draw in the round of 16, they saw off Cote D'Ivoire with Salah saving himself for the final, decisive kick. They won in extra time against Morocco in the next round and then repeated the penalty feat against the hosts in the semi-final, again after a game that yielded no goals in 120 minutes. Cameroon's spot-kicks were laughably inept and Egypt only had to convert three attempts, meaning the great man didn't even need to step up. Given what happened in the same stadium in Yaoundé three days later, he might have done better to have kept his eye in.

In a final billed by commentators from all quarters as Mane vs Salah, Senegal played Egypt in Yaoundé just as the fates had decreed that they would meet in March to play off for a place in Qatar. In the huff and puff of the two hours of play that ensued, Mane had a penalty saved by Mohamed Abou Gabal, who went on to be the busier of the two keepers in a turgid affair witnessed by around 35,000 people – just over half the stadium's capacity. Despite a significant Senegalese community in Cameroon and the influx of dozens of flights from Egypt, a combination of high prices, Covid restrictions and continued anxiety in the wake of the fatal crush accounted for this disappointing turnout. They watched on as, once again, penalties were to be taken after the game produced no goals.

Senegal scored three of their first four, Egypt two of their first three. They needed to score their fourth to level things up and, in effect, keep themselves in the contest. They must have been relieved at their tactical nous in keeping the main man back to take this crucial kick. Except he didn't. Up stepped Mohanad Lasheen of Tala'ea El Gaish from Egypt's Premier League to slap an ineffectual effort close enough for Chelsea's Edouard Mendy to pretty well fall over and easily bat it away. Sadio Mane then made up for his miss earlier in the game and Senegal's entire squad dutifully raced across the turf like men on fire, leaving one of the world's top strikers bemused in the centre circle, having been unable to use his considerable skill to affect the result. His Liverpool team-mate attempted to console him, but it's difficult to imagine that he didn't ask him what the bloody hell he was playing at.

A few weeks later, when the footballing gods had decreed that the two teams be drawn against each other in the play-off for a place at Qatar, Salah had learnt his lesson. With the two-leg tie once again going to penalties, he elected to take the first kick in the ensuing shoot-out. Whether the use of laser-pen from the crowd had any effect, or if it was just the accumulation of doubt from events in Yaoundé, he lofted his penalty way over the bar and then watched as his Liverpool buddy sealed the tie. Salah may not have thought so at the time, but Mane's triumphant moment was one to be relished by football followers around the globe.

Sadio Mane is one of the modern game's true role models. In December 2020 a photo emerged of him carrying an iPhone with a cracked screen, something which appeared to bother his followers and supporters much more deeply than himself. This transgression against behavioural norms was unsurprising. Some months earlier he had told TeleDakar in his homeland that the trappings of stardom held limited appeal. 'Why would I want ten Ferraris, 20 diamond watches and two jet planes?' he asked. 'I prefer to build schools and give poor people clothing and food ... I prefer that my people receive a little of what life has given me.' He's as good as his word, having financed a hospital, sports facilities and schools, as well as providing regular financial maintenance for those in the region of his remote village birthplace of Bambali.

AFCON drew to its conclusion and the Beijing Winter Olympics began. Now, at the risk of undermining any unlikely sales of this book in the People's Republic, I'll express the uncontroversial view that if you're looking at Sports Mega Events held in oppressive, brutal regimes, you don't just need to focus on hangers, floggers and choppers in the Middle East. As well as its secretive and chilling use of the death penalty, one of China's most notorious and public human rights abuses takes place in the Xinjiang region in the northwest of the country, where Uyghur Muslims are detained, 're-educated' and, according to credible reports, subjected to the forced use of contraception and sterilization.

The reaction of Western powers to this egregious situation has been forceful, dynamic and direct: some of them enforced a full diplomatic boycott of the winter games. Yes, you read that correctly: a full – in most cases, that is – diplomatic boycott. The games, you understand, went ahead and athletes from around the world competed, it's just that they'll have to do so without the support of their country's diplomats roaring them on from behind the glass of the corporate boxes. The extent to which their performances were affected was genuinely inestimable.

None of this official timidity is remotely surprising, given sports' rulers weak-kneed approach to calling out injustice. The Uyghur Muslim story had attracted a degree of attention in the UK media, but it was brought to greater prominence by the intervention of a footballer, Arsenal's Mesut Ozil. In December 2019 he had tweeted his disappointment at the reaction of governments not just in the West, but also from the Muslim world. 'Where are Muslims?' he asked to a chorus of spluttering disapproval from a footballing world that still hadn't been forced into acknowledging that taking the knee wasn't part of a Marxist-Leninist putsch. His employers, who had other beef with him about tracking back and picking up his runner, acted swiftly. They issued a post on Weibo, a Chinese social media site, ensuring their distance from their player's comments. 'Regarding the comments made by Mesut Ozil on social media, Arsenal must make a clear statement,' it read. 'The content published is Ozil's personal opinion. As a football club, Arsenal has always adhered to the principle of not involving itself in politics.'

It's unfair to single out the Arsenal (I'm sorry to say). A similarly flaccid response was on show in Australia just as AFCON swung into the knockout stages and the fake, allegedly eco-friendly, snow in Beijing was being ploughed into place. During the weeks prior to the Australian Open tennis tournament, the country's government had stood firm, faced off legal challenges and seen through its threat to deport the unvaccinated Novak Djokovic. That was about as far as its muscle-flexing went. Hanging over the whole competition was smell emanating from the absence of Chinese player Peng Shuai.

In November 2021, Peng Shuai had made an accusation of sexual assault against a senior Chinese official, Zhang Gaoli. There followed a period during which her whereabouts were unknown and concern for her safety expressed – only for these to be addressed by a series of dodgy, staged video clips of her looking cringingly uncomfortable at public events. This video evidence did nothing to allay the concerns of the Women's

Tennis Association, who undertook not to play in China in 2022. They were not alone in wishing to express their disapproval. Protesters in Melbourne turned up to the arena sporting tee-shirts featuring a photo of Peng on the front below the word 'wanted'. On the back was the question, 'Where is Peng Shuai?' They were immediately accosted by security guards who insisted that they either remove the shirts or be ejected from the stadium.

After its effective posturing in supporting its government over the Djokovic case, Tennis Australia seemed to have run out of nerve. 'Under our ticket conditions of entry we don't allow clothing, banners or signs that are commercial or political ... Peng Shuai's safety is our primary concern. We continue to work with the global tennis community to seek more clarity on her situation and will do everything we can to ensure her wellbeing.' Their statement remained stubbornly quiet about maintaining good relations with one of the Open's major commercial sponsors, Chinese premium liquor brand Guojiao 1573.

SMEs and protest. As far as could be discerned, AFCON, notwithstanding military coups, stampedes and some abnormally inefficient refereeing, seemed to be free of any incident. Stay-away diplomats hardly had China quaking in its boots and the cowed genuflection of Tennis Australia wouldn't have given Xi Jinping and his buddies any sleepless nights. The hurricane of

Russia's invasion of Ukraine and the reaction of the football world and, eventually, FIFA had yet to really shake the ground beneath all our feet. So, looking at AFCON, Beijing and the Australian Open, what might have been in the thoughts of the great and the good in Doha? Who might be around to try to embarrass them? And, crucially, with millions more eyes on them than on the tennis or the curling, how would they choose to deal with public dissent?

Chapter 10

I'd keep that to yourself, if I were you. Could a World Cup really challenge ideas about equality?

A PICTURE of Trevor Francis in the classic blue-and-white penguin shirt adorns the wall of my downstairs toilet – yes, I'm that posh. He was indisputably the best Birmingham City player I have ever seen and, although it seems possible that Jude Bellingham may yet outstrip his achievements, the youngster's exploits with us were all too fleeting. Trevor – he requires no other identification – was a sublime player but a mediocre manager. I've always thought him fortunate because one exceptional blunder has, by and large, not quite haunted him as terrifyingly as it might have done. It was his Dick Rowe moment which occurred during his time in charge at Sheffield Wednesday.

Dick Rowe was the agent from Decca records who famously turned down the Beatles because he saw them going nowhere. For Lennon and McCartney, read Eric Cantona. Trevor was given first dibs on this celestial talent, but, having only seen him train on astroturf, wanted to see him on grass before committing to anything.

Eric didn't take too kindly to this and threw in his lot with Wednesday's neighbours at Leeds where, it might be fair to say, he made something of an impact. He became truly world-famous as a player and, latterly, as an actor, campaigner and ... well, just being Eric Cantona. I'm not going to go all postmodern about this, but part of Cantona's undoubted genius is that he now makes a significant impact by being Eric Cantona playing various versions of Eric Cantona.

Just as the tight-lipped Eddie Howe was planning Newcastle's great escape with some paint-balling and set-piece drills in Saudi's winter sunshine, Cantona took to the airwaves and the ether to speak out about what was to happen in the region later in the year. 'To be honest, I don't really care about the next World Cup, which is not a real World Cup for me,' he told the *Daily Mail*. He went on to express the view that Qatar was 'not the country of football' before venturing into the territory of workers' rights. 'It's only about money and the way they treated the people who built the stadiums, it's horrible. And thousands of people died. And yet we will celebrate this World Cup.'

If the musings of moody Eric were music to the ears of the journos at the happily and perennially xenophobic *Mail*, their counterparts in Doha were not going to be quite so pliable. The former French international had been happy enough to watch matches in Russia, pointed out the *Doha News*. 'Boycotts in the previous World Cups in Russia and Brazil were not seriously discussed,' it pointed out, 'despite both nations having a poor track record when it comes to human rights.' Maybe, the paper suggested, 'recent calls for a boycott of Qatar 2022 are part of a wider smear campaign against Doha'. The *News* tetchily cited local academic Dr Justin Martin, who had tweeted that it was 'hard to take him seriously since he promoted WC in Russia, where LGBTQ symbols are illegal, journalists are routinely jailed, and protestors are beaten and disappeared'.

In the same bullish vein, the *News* took major issue with Cantona's claims that there was little footballing culture in Qatar, dismissing his comments as part of the continuing trend of a 'deficient Western gaze'. There had, the paper insisted, been such a tradition since 1948 'when oil workers organised matches amongst themselves … generations both young and old are seen playing the sport in parks and schools alike, and the Qatari national team has won the Arabian Gulf Cup three times, in addition to the first AFC Asian Cup'. The former striker's reactions to these comments were not sought, which is a bit of shame for those of us who might have enjoyed the journalistic equivalent of a kung-fu leap into the air-conditioned offices of complacent pen-pushers.

The Qatari newspaper's ripostes stood, of course, in the proper tradition of robust journalism and were entirely legitimate – welcome, even, in the spirit of open debate. Anticipating what was likely to become a growing discourse around protest and dissent, this first step into the tedious see-sawing of whataboutery was entirely predictable. In comparison to what was going on some 4,000 miles to the east, this warning to potential purveyors of protest was the very model of gentility and temperance.

As athletes and reporters began to gather in Beijing, the Chinese authorities issued warnings that had all the messaging subtlety of a brick through the window at midnight. 'Any behaviour or speech that is against the Olympic spirit, especially against the Chinese laws and regulations, are subject to certain punishment,' Yang Shu, the deputy director of Beijing's Olympic organizing committee, warned during a call organised by the Chinese embassy in Washington. These were not just empty words. With the games taking place in three Covid bubbles and under close physical guard, all those inside a particular bubble were mandated to download the 'My2022' app, ostensibly to monitor their health and their movements between venues. The security of the encryption of the app aroused immediate and authoritative suspicion.

A report from the University of Toronto expressed the concern that 'such data can be read by any passive eavesdropper, such as someone in range of an unsecured wifi access point, someone operating a wifi hotspot, or an internet service provider or other telecommunications company'. Put more simply, the app could easily expose personal data, compromising the privacy and security of senders and recipients of messages. With widespread evidence of routine suppression of dissent in China, from the hounding of academics to the imprisonment of activists and the hacking of social media accounts, it was clear that the state authorities had no intention of allowing athletes to use the games as a platform from which to make any controversial statements. Given a longstanding track record of harassing through to disappearing, it'd be a pretty committed snowboarder who wanted to seize the moment and call out Xi Jinping and his big brothers.

Eager to impress its growing ease with aspects of Western liberalism, Qatar and its various authorities did not seem to be looking at the Chinese model as any sort of template when it came to quashing dissent. But, having understood football's close relationship with alcohol for many of its global supporters and having demonstrated a willingness to accommodate this, there remained one area of immense cultural and religious importance that needed to be addressed – its attitude to, and potential tolerance of, people from the LGBTQ+ communities. As always, it might be worth reflecting for a moment or two on the tidiness of our own house before squinting into someone else's front room.

In February 2022, Channel 4 broadcast the documentary *Football's Coming Out.* Broadly optimistic in tone, it interviewed players, ex-players, managers and agents from all levels of the game. All were agreed that football dressing rooms, notwithstanding the ruthless 'banter' that characterises them from the Prem to the parks, reflected society's growing broad-mindedness when it came to gay footballers in both the men's and women's game. The enduringly optimistic Ian Holloway talked of how he would have been flattered had a player placed sufficient trust in him to have told him of his sexuality. Joleon Lescott and Patrick Bamford, neither of them strangers to Neanderthal crowd baiting, expressed concern about terrace reaction, but were confident that change was on the way.

Matt Morton, the openly gay player-manager of Thetford Town in level nine of the English pyramid, is the most highly paid player in the current game to come out – 'and look at me,' he grins. 'I'm hardly Cristiano Ronaldo'. Reflecting on the stubborn fact that there is no single footballer playing at the higher levels in England who has chosen to come out, Morton is confident in his assertion that there must be a fair number concealing their sexuality, albeit for understandable reasons.

For all its obvious efforts to convince the world that it understands their concerns about Qatar's illiberalism, the use of the lash and the sword for perceived sexual misconduct still linger in popular Western imagination. When it comes to the law of the land, there is good news and bad news. Written edicts may be stringent and frightening, but punishments, particularly for non-Muslims and non-residents, are less chilling. Nonetheless, erring very heavily on the side of caution would still seem to be the sensible thing to do.

The letter of the law is unequivocal. Technically, gay people could find entry to the country troublesome. Article 25 of law no 21 of 2015 allows for ministerial power to order an expatriate to leave the country on moral grounds. Based on this law, the government could prevent LGBTQ+ people from entering or deport them on the grounds of their sexual orientation. Sexual acts between people of the same sex are illegal under article 296(3) of the Penal Code. What's more, anything that encourages same sex relationships, including assemblies, publications or associations, are considered to be promoting a criminal offence and are prohibited. Under the same article, punishments include imprisonment for between one and five years. Sharia courts also exist where, theoretically, it is possible that Muslim men could be face the death penalty for same-sex activity.

The good news is that even without the eyes of the world directed towards it, many of these punishments are more honoured in the breach than the observance. The international group ILGA (International Lesbian, Gay, Bisexual, Trans and Intersex Association) along with other campaigners such as Stonewall and Amnesty, remain confident that no death penalty has been imposed for this reason. Figures for other corporal punishments are impossible to obtain but evidence seems to suggest that instances of its use are extremely rare.

Eager to reassure potential visitors, a press conference in early 2022 saw Nassar al-Khater, the chief executive of the organising committee, telling journalists that he 'would like to assure any fan, of any gender, sexual orientation, religion or race to rest assured that Qatar is one of the most safe countries in the world – and they'll all be welcome here'. For those of us used to matchday security carried out by bored 17-year-olds on minimum wage and in a high-viz designed for much burlier versions of themselves, Al-Khater's further guarantee that 'there's a lot of training going into security personnel to make sure that things that are culturally different are seen in that frame' didn't really cut much ice. He went on to warn that 'public displays of affection are frowned upon, it's not part of our culture – but that goes across the board to everybody'. He didn't specify whether that included draping yourself drunkenly across your companion and telling them that they were your best mate, but I'm guessing we can take that as read.

Which is not an attempt to trivialise an alarming situation. I am indebted to the dedication of journalist David Harding whose work for *The Independent* newspaper gave a voice to gay people from Qatar, albeit an anonymised one, in his series of articles and podcasts in the two years or so leading up to the World Cup. It's a dispiriting picture. In a particularly telling conversation, a well-educated and articulate gay man talks of how he persuaded himself to elect for a university course in the more 'manly' subject of engineering, rather than following his interests in the arts and culture, deemed a more feminine and, as such, 'suspicious' area. Fictitious dates with fictitious girlfriends are also part of his consistent performance of 'normality' where, for all its attempts to downplay it, the notion of homosexuality as an undisputed sin dominates public discourse. In the light of this unrelenting opprobrium, there is nothing approaching a gay community in Qatar, just a collection of disparate individuals. Another Qatari tells Harding that this lack of communal support is disappointing. 'I wish there was such a community,' he explains, 'because it's something I have thought of, to have an inclusive support group system, where it can be easier to feel supported.'

The mixture of anxiety, despair and anger of Harding's interviewees is not born of paranoia. The dating apps Grindr and Tinder are available but generally avoided for fear of contact being detected by the Criminal Investigation Department, which is known to lurk on such platforms. Foreigners and ex-pats have become as savvy as locals when it comes to necessary caution when using the apps. In a rather cheeky, if convoluted, twist, many gay users still use straight apps in the hope of locating like-minded companions. In the non-digital world, an attempt to establish 'safe cafes' was short-lived as they were widely believed to be infiltrated by government spies.

For many gay men in Qatar, the option of a 'lavender wedding', one in which the sexuality of the bride or groom – or both – is concealed in the interests of public approval, is the only viable option. In the face of such drastic action and the avalanche of official disapproval, it is little wonder that Harding had little difficulty in detecting overwhelming anger among gay people in the country. This is further reinforced by what is perceived as startling double-standards among the country's elite. More than happy to court gay celebrities and top-end fashion brands with strong gay connections, this is seen by many as intolerable hypocrisy. 'All financially privileged people here love to buy from "gay brands" … they are brought to life by the gays,' an interviewee tells

Harding. 'Qatar supports LGBT products in secret and arrest LGBT out in the open.'

The constant reassurances afforded to the outside world about the safety of gay people at the World Cup constitutes a strong insult to locals. It is summed up by the complaint of another anonymous respondent, who decries that fact that 'temporary and conditional tolerance only to meet the standard of FIFA during the World Cup is hypocritical and disgusting.' How come a taboo subject, which is criminalised by religion and law suddenly become tolerable? We are human too and this protection should stay after the World Cup.' Talk of rainbow flags, laces and armbands seems welcome enough and, perhaps, will be the extent of any likely protest during the competition itself. For gay people in Qatar, who are not looking for 'Western saviours', this will only be viewed as the slightest contribution to a much more protracted and demanding march toward progress.

Don't kiss, don't hold hands. Wear a flag or a tee-shirt if you must. Comply with these low-key demands and you're almost sure to get home safely … and, to be entirely fair, the same pretty much applies to Molineux as to the Al Janoub. Qatar seems determined to adopt something of a 'don't ask, don't tell' policy towards this challenge to the country's customs and laws. Come to the game, enjoy our sanitised hospitality and don't spoil it by

Embarrassing snaps from the past. Infantino and Putin have a little cuddle.

200,000 people witness the Maracanazo. Uruguay 2, Brazil 1 in 1950. Suicide attempts followed Brazil's defeat.

The African star of the non-African World Cup. Eusebio takes a tumble against North Korea in 1966 – he gets up to score from the spot.

Henry Kissinger (far right) with US President Richard Nixon and Golda Meir, Israeli President in 1973. 'The politics of soccer make me nostalgic for the politics of the Middle East.'

Der Kaiser, Franz Beckenbauer, strides forward imperiously. Best to remember him this way before he started doing deals.

Roger Milla heads off to dance with the corner flag after scoring against Colombia in 1990. Goal celebrations were never the same again.

Blatter pulls it out. Any banknotes left in that envelope? Just kidding.

Migrant workers' accommodation in Doha in 2012. Assurances were given that improvements would be made.

German players line up prior to their qualifier with Iceland. Qatar authorities will be hoping for no such repeats this winter.

Victorious Algerian players carry the flag of Palestine during the Arab Cup in Doha.

Italian players protest after Bryan Moreno sends off Totti in 2002. A ref you'd definitely like to see operating under VAR.

Partying on the beach. A tradition that the Qataris might not take to with enthusiasm.

Cyle Larin celebrates after scoring for Canada in their qualifier against USA. His team could be the surprise package of the World Cup.

Nasser al-Khelaifi in contemplative mood. Possibly thinking about how his numerous interests will be piling up the cash.

Anti-logos aimed at the main sponsors started cropping up over the internet as soon as Qatar's successful bid was announced.

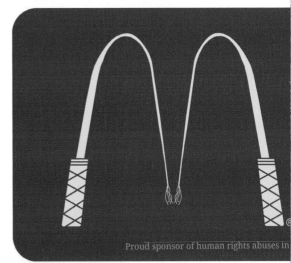

Proud sponsor of human rights abuses in

Hot dog and chips at the match – and the chance that you'll get to touch the ball. Football that's a million miles from the corporate circus.

being awkward. When it comes to women supporters, it's not much different.

The Expatica website provides an illuminating guide to women's rights in Qatar. From the start, it makes it plain that, in many respects, the country, existing 'right at the intersection of modernity and tradition', rates highly within the Gulf in respect of women's rights. It talks of a generalised respect for women in society and of how harassment or catcalling in public are virtually unknown. There are significant numbers of women graduates and it is possible to own a business and to serve in local government, albeit on a co-opted, rather than a democratically elected, basis. Dress codes, particularly for foreigners, do not prohibit shorts or short skirts, although an emphasis on general modesty is prevalent in all available advice. Balanced against this, legislation remains firmly in place which makes male guardianship mandatory in many aspects of life, most notably in terms of travel and choice of marriage partners. Domestic violence and marital rape are not criminalized and divorce, although available, almost always favours men in terms of outcomes such as finance and custody of children. Although it is increasingly acceptable to publicly discuss improving the role of women in society, there exists no independent or governmental bodies dedicated to doing so.

Now, I've made reference to this in another publication, but it remains relevant. My season ticketed seat at St Andrew's is adjacent to the away supporters. I'm not suggesting for a moment that supporters of my own club are endowed with any greater wit and wisdom than those who gather to my left, but week after week you can play a sort of away-supporters' bingo as they blurt out the regulation unoriginals. Old favourites are, as invoked earlier, 'Birmingham's a Shithole, I Want to Go Home' along with 'Is This a Library?' to 'Shall We Sing a Song for You?' and that old standard, 'How Shit Must You Be, We're Winning Away?' From time to time, should a hapless female be spotted among home supporters, we go back to the dark ages of 'Get Yer Tits Out For the Lads' or 'She's Got Chlamydia'. Classy.

The point being that even though such clodhopping sexism is on the wane, it's still there and is reflective of a society that's got some way to go before branding itself as entirely equal. I'm not suggesting that the repression and institutionalised sexism of the Qatari system is replicated in the UK. Neither do I think the vast majority of fans still endorse the worst excesses of sexist chants and attitudes. I'm also not challenging the sanctity of going to football as the bolthole where we can leave the trappings of civilised behaviour and the worries of the wider world behind while we spend afternoons and evening talking complete bollocks. I am merely putting forward the proposition that if, by thinking about Qatari attitudes to women, football fans here begin to reflect on their own conduct, then there could be a real benefit from that introspection. And, no, I'm not holding my breath.

My best guess, writing eight months before kick-off, is that a good deal of blind-eye turning from Qatari officialdom will result in any open protest about sexuality and women's rights being very low-key, if it becomes public at all. A big part of me hopes I'm entirely incorrect. But if it should take place, its importance and impact will only be judged if it brings about changes to attitudes and legislation once the circus has packed up and left town. In the next chapter I'll do some crystal-ball gazing about where a cup winner may come from. I probably won't even bet on my own recommendation, but I certainly wouldn't put any money on Qatar's tournament being the catalyst for a challenge to that country's societal ideas and values. And, once again, I hope I'm completely wrong.

Chapter 11

Picking a winner. History, geography, long odds, hitting the inside of the post and staying out

WINNING A football tournament is difficult to do. Given the number of teams who enter competitions around the globe, the number who eventually end up lifting silverware remains stubbornly limited, especially when it comes to the very top contests. In domestic terms, a good deal of this is accounted for by the virtuous circle of success on the pitch attracting wealthy sponsors of varying integrity. These trusty lovers of the game then ensure that good players are hoovered away from any potential competitors, thereby guaranteeing the continuing success of their various playthings. In internationals teams, the difficulty of breaking into these elites is less easy to explain, although being around the best performers every day in football clubs often prompts, as in any walk of life, the phenomenon of a rising tide floating all ships.

As every schoolchild knows, football was invented in England in 1992. By then, the Premier League had successfully airbrushed all previous history and knowledge except for England's glorious World Cup win in 1966. In the 28 seasons since its inception, four clubs – Arsenal, Chelsea, Manchester United and Manchester City – have won 25 titles between them. During that same period, those four clubs have won 23 FA Cup finals and, just for good measure, even in the relatively unloved and multi-sponsored League Cup, have snaffled 15 of the 28 on offer. Honours in Europe's top club competition have been a touch more evenly spread. There have been 13 separate winners, with Barcelona and their friendly rivals at Real Madrid picking up the trophy 11 times. At international level, it has been less of a closed shop since 1992, with only Spain winning the Euros on more than one occasion, along with some glorious uncertainty raising its head with the successes of Greece and Denmark.

Outside Europe, the winners of international competitions present less of a mixed picture. In the Copa America, Brazil have won five of the last 12 competitions with four other countries dividing the remaining spoils. While Egypt and Cameroon have won seven of the 15 Africa Cup of Nations, other successes have been evenly distributed among a further seven countries. But when it comes to World Cup success, it's a European and South American closed shop.

In its 21 tournaments, there have been South American winners on nine occasions, with Brazil taking five trophies and Uruguay and Argentina two each. Eight of Europe's 12 victories are accounted for by four wins each for Germany and Italy. France has won twice, with one victory each for Spain and England (did anyone mention that England once won the World Cup?) That's a total of eight winners in the history of the competition. Only two African nations, Cameroon in 1990 and Senegal in 2002, have gone as far as the last eight, a success they share with the 1966 North Koreans, albeit that the latter had to play one game fewer to reach that stage. That remained the pinnacle of achievement for Asian teams until 2002, when South Korea went one better to reach the semi-finals, losing to the eventual beaten finalists, Germany, and going on to lose the third-place play-off – the most unwanted, anticlimactic fixture in world football – to Turkey. Of the scores of nations that enter this competition, the same victors keep doggedly reappearing. Might December in the desert disrupt the established order? Could this, perhaps, be Africa's moment.

Before venturing into anything like a serious analysis of this important question, it's worth a digression to look at a couple of features of the game in Africa that always bring a smile and some energy to football. These serve as reminders that despite the grinding disappointment that the game regularly provides – more for some of us than others – it can be a thing of great joy and beauty. The first of these is the nicknames that African national teams take to themselves. There has been some attempt in recent years to emulate this in Europe and elsewhere, most parochially in the adoption of the Three Lions tag for England, a label made particularly poignant when applied as a mark of support for the penalty missers in the Euros final in 2021. But it's pale fare when placed next to its African counterparts.

The Indomitable Lions of Cameroon would have been miffed at having to watch the AFCON final being played between Egypt's Pharaohs and Senegal's Lions of Teranga on their home territory. These lions were not to be confused with Morocco's Atlas Lions, the Leopards of DR Congo or the Panthers of Gabon. One can't help feeling that those who named Cote D'Ivoire and Guinea the Elephants and the National Elephants respectively, might have opted for a beast more renowned for its speed and athleticism, but with Mali having nabbed Eagles and Tunisia bearing the mantle of the even more exotic Eagles of Carthage, it may have been that they were left with the last knockings. The providers of AFCON's biggest upset, Comoros, operate under the banner of the

Coelacanths, which, to save you the google, are fish living almost exclusively off the coast of the islands.

There is another area where one African player in particular brought something to the game that has made its imprint on every game of football played anywhere, at any level, across the globe. The barmy goal celebration. As part of the demanding in-depth research which I have applied to the writing of this book, I spent a happy couple of hours watching YouTube clips ensuring that I was not bringing false memory to this. I was not.

The 1990 World Cup was played in Italy and could be considered the turning point for football's respectability after a dark and disturbing period. The palaces of delight that pass for Premier League stadia belong to a different planet from the crumbling, unsafe death-traps of the 70s and 80s. And while football crowds remain largely male and, depending on where you go, working class, there is a degree of civility in evidence that was entirely lacking in the period that culminated in the horrors of Hillsborough and Heysel. But Italia 90 was bright and engaging and England weren't a total disaster. We were enjoying it. And we were especially enjoying Cameroon's Indomitable Lions.

In the opening game of the tournament, Cameroon pulled off one of the greatest shocks in the tournament's history by defeating reigning champions Argentina 1-0 in the San Siro. Once again, time watching the highlights is a rewarding experience. Although moving gradually towards the more genteel, almost non-contact sport of the 21st century, football in 1990 was still a spirited, physical affair, even at the highest level. It's fair to say that Argentina, themselves no strangers to the grittier side of the game, were somewhat caught out by the uncompromising approach of their relatively unknown opponents. Given the unlost love for the South Americans and Cameroon's agricultural attitude to parts of the beautiful game, they almost immediately became everyone's second team. This love was firmly cemented a few days later in Bari's Stadio San Nicola.

Playing Romania or, in the preferred terminology of commentators with a fixed agenda, Gheorghe Hagi's Romania, Cameroon carried on from the Argentina game, flying into everything with beefy abandon, leavened by plenty of skill and tactical awareness. On 58 minutes, with the game goalless, they brought on 38-year-old Roger Milla. He was lithe and athletic and looked as if he'd been hewn out of stone and, frankly, he could conceivably have been any age from 25 to 45. Fourteen minutes after coming on, he bullied his way past his defender to bring a bouncing ball under control and neatly slot it past the advancing keeper. Eight minutes later, from around the same spot, he absolutely lashed an unstoppable shot into the roof of the net and, despite Romania pulling one back with two minutes to go ensured that Cameroon would go to the last 16 in the competition. They were two wonderful goals, but it was what he did after both that really imprinted his name on the game's history.

Once again, I double checked some footage to ensure there was no false memory involved in the telling of this tale. Before I did so, however, I can reliably call on my own spectating experience to establish immediate context. It was probably around the early 70s when, for whatever reason, the firm handshake or, at the very worst, an arm round the shoulder or a ruffle of the hair started giving way to more demonstrative shows of congratulation, affection even, among players. In the distinctly unsentimental and unamorous surroundings of Birmingham City's Spion Kop, such manifestations did not go down well, especially if exhibited by opposition players. 'Go on then, sweetie. Give him a fucking kiss, then,' might have been typical of the reaction in those unreconstructed, unenlightened days.

By way of an aside gleaned from my other sporting love, I checked on footage that I'd dimly remembered of Jim Laker, the England bowler, picking up 19 of the 20 wickets in the Ashes Test match at Old Trafford in 1956. Even as he completed the feat, his team-mates clapped briefly and politely, there was one restrained half-jump for joy, a few handshakes and that was it. No snarling, no send-off, no wild circling of the playing area, no eyes to heaven … nothing. Much the same applied to football and even when the kissing and cuddling was well entrenched by the 1980s, the days of the choreographed, incomprehensible goal celebration were still very much a thing of the future. And the man who changed it was 25-to-45-year-old Roger Milla of Cameroon.

On scoring his first goal at the San Nicola, Milla charged off joyfully and headed straight for the corner flag. Once there, he used it as an inanimate dancing partner while he performed a hip-wiggling fandango around it. By the standards set since, it looks charmingly tame, but this was something very new. When he repeated it after the second goal, we were entranced and wanted to see it again. We didn't get to do so in the final group match, by now meaningless for Cameroon with six points. His team was thumped 4-0 by the Soviet Union, but in the first knock-out game we were twice treated to the jiggle against Colombia. The second was a gift from another player whose antics have written him into the game's folklore – goalkeeper Rene Higuita, known for very good reason as El Loco.

On this occasion, Higuita, imagining himself as a ball-playing libero, came some 20 yards from his area, attempted to beat the onrushing Milla with some nifty footwork and, on clumsily surrendering possession, was forced to watch helplessly as the forward cheerily escorted the ball into an empty net. However, it was not solely this gaffe that cemented El Loco's reputation; it was his execution of the mind-boggling scorpion kick to save a shot from Jamie Redknapp at Wembley in 1995 that was indisputably unique. Walk past any kickabout anywhere in the world and it's a good bet that somebody, somewhere will be giving it a go. One can only imagine that a night out with Milla and Higuita might have been a lively affair.

Milla did not come on until the second half in the quarter-final game against England in Naples, a contest decided by two nerveless penalties by Gary Lineker, who was once quite a good footballer before he became properly famous as a woke, lefty pundit. Cameroon have never progressed beyond the group stages since then and have not qualified since 2014, although they have won AFCON on three occasions. Their achievement in reaching the last eight – and very nearly progressing from there – was not equalled until Senegal did the same in 2002. They were captained by the admirable (and ex-Birmingham favourite) Aliou Cisse, who then managed them to AFCON victory against Egypt in January and then to the pay-off triumph against the same opponents in Dakar in March. In the end, the continent's five places at Qatar were filled by Cisse's men along with Tunisia, Ghana, Cameroon and Morocco.

Do any of these countries stand any chance of breaking into the winners' enclosure? Simple arithmetic places them at an immediate disadvantage. With 54 FIFA members, CAF, the African federation, is allocated its five places in the finals. Europe, via UEFA, has 55 members with 13 allocations. On top of this, history is clearly not on their side. Despite some moments of expectation, all have remained unfulfilled since Cameroon's initial breakthrough in 1990. Analysis of why this should be is varied, inconclusive and often tinged with racism.

In an otherwise serious attempt to discuss the situation, an article in *Goal* magazine in May 2020 talked of how, in a transfer market that scours the globe for potential talent, 'from Africa, it appears it is the brawny midfielder with an iron lung that is prized above all'. There's probably an entirely different book to be written about the preconceptions about that single observation. Less controversially, it is now universally accepted that any element of surprise that might once have emanated from those playing in more distant parts of the world is a thing of the past. Nigerian football historian Calvin Onwuka told the magazine that with so many of the best African players now playing in the Champions League, there is little chance of their national teams bringing anything out of the ordinary to the World Cup. The effect goes even deeper as both club and national teams from Africa try 'to copy what they consider to be best practice in football by emulating what they see on

TV'. Moreover, the wider implications of young players looking immediately towards Europe for development has obvious ramifications for the growth of the game in their home countries.

Serious academic analysis, as is so often the case when applied to the unpredictable illogicality of football, is unable to provide greater illumination. In 2018, Alliance Kubayi and Abel Toriola from Tshwane University in South Africa completed a comprehensive but unintentionally hilarious statistical analysis of the performance of African teams at the 2018 World Cup in Russia. They concluded, 'European teams had higher averages than African teams on the following performance variables: total shots, shots on target, goals scored from open play and set pieces, ball possession, short passes, medium passes, total passes, accurate passes and corner kicks.' Their principal recommendation was that these were the areas on which coaches of African teams should concentrate for future success. Yep, that should just about cover it.

In citing work from other academics, they talk of the importance of retaining possession. They noted, 'Teams who dominated European competitions adopted a style of play based on a possession style or indirect play, suggesting they preferred to control the game by dictating play' and they advise, 'It is important that African teams should keep possession in order to improve their chances of success.' I might just send that same report to the bloke who sits two rows behind me and has spent the last 20 years (and probably longer) bellowing at our players to 'gerrit forward!'

If it is unlikely that a team from Africa will break the mould, could the East spring a surprise? The closest that ever came to happening was in 2002. The tournament was hosted jointly by Japan and South Korea and, prior to Qatar, it was the only time the event has been held in Asia. Given that much of this book's narrative considers the challenge posed to old orders by emerging football nations, it's worth reflecting on how the finals not only ended up in this part of the world, but on the emerging football pedigree of both host nations.

The world in 2002 had come some way from the genuine but patronising admiration that had been bestowed on those lovable little North Koreans 38 years earlier. Their southern neighbours have now qualified for every tournament since 1986, which has gone some way to eradicating the painful memory of their 9-0 annihilation at the hand of the Magnificent Magyars in Zurich in 1954, their only appearance prior to that. Unbeaten in their qualifiers by the start of February 2022, their place was one of the earliest booked in Qatar. When the joint award for 2002 was made in 1996, their Japanese neighbours had never qualified for the final stages but have gone on to play in every World Cup since 1998.

Both Japan and South Korea had submitted individual bids to host the 2002 event with the only other sombrero in the ring being cast by Mexico. Theirs was never considered a serious effort. In the early stages of the process, they must have looked at the aggressive marketing and PR of both the Asian federations and decided that, what with two World Cups and one Olympics in the previous 24 years already in the bag, they could afford to let this one go – until 2026, of course, when they will be part of the new, shiny 48-team intergalactic soccer special with Canada and the USA. There was no such conciliation between the two remaining protagonists in 2002. With the added spice of Joao Havelange of FIFA making no secret of his support for Japan and UEFA's Lennart Johansson backing the Koreans, there was definitely no regional solidarity on show. Possibly sensing that it couldn't end well, a joint award, the first of its kind, was the outcome. If FIFA thought it had come up with a sensible compromise, it was sorely mistaken.

Kim Ga-young of Korea's bidding committee had either lost or forgotten the memo about magnanimity in victory and grace in defeat. 'This is a victory for us and a loss for Japan,' he told Reuters news agency. 'The Japanese were all along against the idea of co-hosting, but they accepted it at the last minute. We won.' Unsurprisingly, this triumphant abrasiveness was met with equal venom from Kenji Mori, the managing director of Japan's J

League. 'This is the worst-case scenario,' he fumed. 'It's going to be terrible, but we have to think positive.'

And there was, at least, some genuine positivity for both home nations once the football began. Japan ran out comfortable group winners with victories against Russia and Tunisia and a draw against a Belgium team yet to begin their ascent of the world rankings. South Korea were equally impressive with a draw against the United States and victories against Poland and Portugal. Yes, I know: Luis Figo's Portugal. That's when the fun started. Japan fell in the last 16 to an efficient Turkish team that eventually finished third in the competition. South Korea went to Daejeon to play the mighty Italy. They may have been massively unfancied, but they had a card up their sleeve, whether they knew it or not, in the figure of referee Bryan Moreno from Ecuador.

Just to be clear, I hate VAR and I want rid. I still carry enduring, deep-seated grudges against refereeing decisions that I recall from nearly 60 years of watching live football. I'm happy to do so; it makes supporting a team what it is. I have been witness to hundreds, possibly thousands, of egregious errors that have negatively affected my team and, to be entirely even-handed, at least three or four that have impacted on our opponents. You get the picture: moaning about referees and putting up with wrong decisions are part of the fabric of the game. Get on with it. What's that you say? With so much money involved, we have to get things right. Ah, so it's about the money? Silly old me thinking it was about sport and all that it can teach you about life, companionship, victory, defeat and a sense of perspective. Having said all of which – Bryan Moreno, mate: you had a shocker.

He laid out his stall by awarding the softest of penalties to the hosts, with justice being done when it was duly saved. In an episode of comical irony, the Koreans then proceeded to kick and lunge at the Italians – themselves no strangers to football's dark and sneaky arts – becoming ever more confident of avoiding any punishment from the tolerant Moreno as the game wore on. In extra time he gave a second yellow to Francesco Totti for diving when it was touch and go as to whether it was a penalty, and then disallowed what would have been Italy's golden-goal winner. The hosts went on to score a perfectly good goal of their own and progressed to the next round against Spain, where once again some generous officiating saw two seemingly good goals from their opponents disallowed before the Koreans went on to win on penalties. By then, Moreno was on his way home … but not yet out of our story.

In September 2010 he was arrested at New York's Kennedy airport with six kilos of heroin concealed about his person. He made little attempt to protest his innocence and ended up serving two years in prison for his misdemeanours. Unsurprisingly, this caper attracted significant attention in Italy where his performance had embedded itself into that country's football folklore. A strong discourse, or, to be less formal, a colourful conspiracy theory, had taken firm root which asserted that Moreno had been appointed to ensure that, with the elimination of Japan, one of the host nations progressed to the next round. Full-back Christian Panucci expressed the view that 'he was put in place to eliminate Italy', before going on to partially invoke a terrace-chant favourite by pronouncing that 'he was a bandit ... and look at the images – he was too fat to referee'. Veteran goalkeeper Gianluigi Buffon, who had saved the dodgy penalty, took a slightly jollier approach when quipping that Moreno was already in possession of a serious amount of drugs in 2002, 'but not in his underwear – in his system'.

Germany ground out their regulation win against South Korea in the semi-final and the co-hosts suffered a fate similar to their unloved neighbours by going on to lose to Turkey, finishing fourth in the tournament. This remains the pinnacle of achievement for Asian teams in the competition. In the ensuing four tournaments prior to Qatar, South Korea got out of the group stages. In 2010 Japan did so and repeated the feat in 2018. In 2006, Australia, which had been decreed Asian by FIFA, also made it to the last 16. The only team from the Gulf ever to have done so was Saudi Arabia in 1994. Statistics, history and plain old inexperience when it comes to winning, all militate against the possibility of a victor from outside South America or Europe.

Might home advantage and familiarity with conditions have an impact? Probably not, even though winning outside your own continent remains comparatively rare. Brazil have done so on three occasions in 1958, 1994 and 2002, in Sweden, the USA and South Korea respectively. Germany won in Brazil in 2014, having administered another Belo Horizonte moment to rival the USA's 1950 triumph by murdering the hosts 7-1. Spain won in South Africa in 2010. If you don't count Argentina's success in Mexico as having genuinely crossed continents and then apply the same kind of logic to France's triumph in Russia, that's only five occasions out of 21, seven at the outside, that have seen the trophy taking an intercontinental leap.

If Africa and Asia seem unlikely to break the mould, could it be down to the Americas to do so? With 41 associate members, the Confederation of Northern, Central American and Caribbean Association Football (CONACAF) provides at least three qualifiers for the finals. As we go to print, USA, Canada and Mexico have booked their places. Costa Rica, fourth in the qualifying group, will have to wait until June to play off against Oceania winners New Zealand to see if they will be joining them. It's a downward step for the central

Americans. In 2014, before slogging through a miserable 0-0 with haplessly eliminated England, they had made their mark with thrilling victories against heavyweights Uruguay and Italy before losing to the Netherlands on penalties in the last eight. Now, along with Wales, Scotland and Ukraine, they will have to wait to see if they'll be joining the fun – a chillingly inappropriate term to use in the same breath as the last of those nations.

Serial achievers USA, despite a blip in not qualifying in 2018, have progressed beyond the group stage in three out of six attempts since 1990. They now find themselves in the same qualifying group as England, prepared to invoke the ghosts of Belo Horizonte and Rob Green. With them sit Canada, at whom we'll look in a moment, and then, almost anomalously, there is Mexico. I'd like to bet that, like me, there are a few readers who thought they must be in with the big boys from South America. Not so.

With two exceptions, Mexico have qualified for every set of finals since 1950. They failed to qualify in 1974, and in 1990 they had been banned from the competition for fielding overage players in the qualifying rounds of the 1988 Olympics. It was the sort of clerical error that might be excusable when made by a bleary-eyed Sunday-league secretary up to her/his knees in registration forms as the clock strikes midnight: less so for an international federation. When they were hosts in 1970 and 1986, they reached the quarter-finals. Other than that, in the very embodiment of a sort of mid-table mediocrity, they have reached the last 16 of the last seven World Cups and progressed no further.

As the final stages for qualification for Qatar approached, they were a respectably solid 12th in the FIFA rankings. However, getting to play what has been dubbed the infamous fifth game, 'el quinto partido' has now assumed the magnitude of a mythological quest. At least veteran right-back Ricardo Osorio managed to put his finger on the problem. Mexican teams in the past 'did not score enough goals to pass to the next round,' he revealed, going on to explain that in future 'that is what [they] will try to do'. It's a simple game, eh?

No team from the Caribbean islands will be in Qatar. I suspect that their absence will rob the event of some of the best potential partying on offer – and probably be greeted with quiet relief by the local authorities. I speak from the experience of two glorious footballing evenings. The first was in Paris in 1998 on the concourse of the Hotel de Ville. Having been unable to get hold of tickets for the game in the nearby Parc des Princes, our travelling company went for what may have been the second-best venue but turned out to be the first-choice party as (Robbie Earle's) Jamaica played Argentina. The predictable 5-0 spanking handed out was practically inconsequential as the summer sky darkened over Paris, its haziness enhanced by the minute in the languid and smokily fragrant evening air.

Eight years later and off on a pilgrimage to Dortmund to enjoy Birmingham City legend Stern John and to barrack pantomime villain Olof Mellberg. On the park, it turned out to be a dull affair, with Trinidad and Tobago and Sweden failing to produce a goal, despite the former playing half the game with ten men. At the final whistle, crowds poured on to the streets for the raucous, good-natured all-nighter that most of them had come for. In terms of cultural adjustment, such an event under the desert moon could well stretch the temporary tolerance of the Qataris. With no Caribbean nations present, it's a test they won't have to take.

The flamboyance of the islands will be absent, replaced by the stolid presence of the sturdy Canadians, who have turned out to be something of surprise package in the qualifying process. Whatever impact they make at the finals, it looks as though it must improve on their current record. Having qualified just the once in 1986, they lost all three group games and failed to score a goal. They didn't quite find themselves in the mandatory group of death, but they had been dealt a tricky hand with games against France, Hungary and the Soviet Union. The weight of history, however, rests lightly on the shoulders of Canada's head coach, John Herdman. In late January 2022, his team beat their noisy American neighbours to go top of the group and almost certainly book themselves a place in the sun. They'll probably recall that decisive, jarring game in Hamilton on the western tip of Lake Ontario when replacing fluids at ten-minute intervals in November.

The wearing of gloves by outfield players is usually regarded in old-school quarters as dubious practice. Anyone watching footage of the Canada-USA game at Tim Hortons Field might want to rethink any lingering prejudice about that: just looking at the video, with fans wrapped up like Michelin men against the icy wind from the lake, induces a shiver. All the same, those same old-schoolers would have nodded in quiet admiration when, four minutes into the freezing start of the game, Canada's Kamal Miller dispelled any possible notions harboured by USA star Christian Pulisic that this was going to be a tiki-taka sort of afternoon. He did, as they say, leave him in no doubt that he was in for a contest.

Having set the tone, a game for the stout-hearted, given free flow by some relaxed refereeing, finished with a 2-0 victory for the home side. Herdman expressed his obvious delight, placing the victory and potential qualification in a broader context. 'We knew we could change a football country forever,' he explained. 'That spirit you see, we all want to get to Qatar. I genuinely believe that these men know they have an opportunity to leave a proper football legacy moving forward.' He's a man you might just trust to do that.

Herdman's coaching trajectory differs from the norm when it comes to international managers. Had Canada ever been tempted to go down the Guus Hiddink route of global gun for hire (Hiddink has plied his trade with seven national teams to go with the same number of clubs) they'll have been pleased to have stuck with the boy from Consett, County Durham. Starting his career as a development officer with Sunderland's youth team, Herdman took his chances by accepting the manager's role with New Zealand's women in 2006. In 2011 he accepted the same post in Canada, almost immediately leading his team to a gold medal in the Pan American Games in Mexico. After bronze medals at the London and Beijing Olympics, he became manager of the men's team. His former charges went on to win gold in Tokyo. When he took over the men's team, they were ranked 95 in the world; after the victory against the USA in the cutting wind of Ontario, they were 33rd. Unlikely winners in Qatar, perhaps, but in a world of changing football influence, Canada could yet be a major player.

But for all of that, the winner will almost certainly come from either Europe or South America. As the qualification process drew to a close in Spring 2022, that most reliable of lodestars which guides the way to football's outcomes, the bookkeeping fraternity, remained resolutely unmoved by any romantic notions emanating from Africa, Asia or the Americas. Brazil, Italy, France,

Spain and Germany hovered in the uncertainty of the pre-tournament air at odds of anything between 7- and 10-1. England, of course, remained snugly in the middle of the pack, always worth 50p of anyone's money for an each-way bet to fall near a final hurdle.

Despite the bookies' efforts, romance remains in the game and the death of Jimmy Greaves in 2021 was a poignant moment for a huge number of football supporters. One of the bitter-sweet treats following his demise was plenty of footage of him gliding over pitches composed of mud, slime, whitewash and water, evading the muscular challenges of yesteryear before lovingly caressing the deadweight of the caseball into the corner of the net. Best to remember him for this consummate skill, because we all – guilty, m'lord – decided it was time to do our 'funny old game' impersonation. Yet, hackneyed as it is, it's true: it's a funny old game. Hit the post at one end, the ball's up the other in a flash for a goal. Should have been 2-0, it's 1-1. And you know you're going to lose. Except sometimes you don't. You can't tell. Because it's a funny old game, and at the top level it's a game decided by millimetres.

In almost all major football tournaments, the better teams get to the final stages. Once there, for all the refinement of marginal gains, sports psychology and muscle memory, a keeper will make a wonder block at one end and 15 seconds later a deflected shot goes in at the other. Miraculous saves, inexplicable misses, fluffed penalties, red mists and moments of sublime brilliance all change games, especially the biggest of games, in a nanosecond. It's how football works.

You want to pick a winner? It'll almost certainly be one of the usual suspects. The bookies will be right. But along the way, a fingertip save, a hothead's clumsy tackle, an inexplicable shank in front of goal or a fat ref, with or without – heaven help us – VAR, will have played their part. Because, despite all the attempt to marketise, sanitise and make it fit for the corporate world, it stubbornly remains a funny old game.

Chapter 12

Who's footing the bill? A World Cup paid for by bottles of pop, cheap TVs and China's soft(ish) global influence

ARSENE WENGER is currently chief of FIFA's global development department. One expects that he brings to that position the same thoroughness and dedication that he did to his 22 years of success and achievement at Arsenal. Nobody in the game seriously doubts that he revolutionised much of what happened in English football, and nowhere was that more immediately apparent than in his attitude to his players' diet. This attracted a mixture of mirth and resistance when he arrived, but is now remarkable only for the fact that it took this well-publicised intervention to drag footballers away from practices that seem utterly bizarre to a modern observer.

Wenger landed at Highbury with an unremarkable managerial record and only the slightest of professional playing credentials. He wore big glasses and spoke in a reserved and measured way, so, obviously, he was 'professorial'. His analytical approach to training and tactics reinforced this learned persona. But it was the food that raised the eyebrows.

Early reports of his being aghast at players standing around on tired legs drinking alcohol after games were confirmed when it then transpired that he had prohibited salt, sugar and … worst of all … chips from the kitchens at the club's training ground. Chips for energy, surely? Like chocolate and jellybeans? Afraid not, boys. It was pasta and plain chicken all the way, chewed slowly. Stories abound of notices around the walls reminding players to do this. Once eaten, this fuel was washed down with plain old water, sipped not slurped. Along with stretching, warming down and, of course, a ban on alcohol – at least where he could see it – this new regime took some time to become accepted. Success on the pitch, however, soon achieved a buy-in from players. Once they had got beyond smuggling in chocolate bars, they began to realise what Wenger was up to. 'What he did,' recalls full-back Nigel Winterburn, 'was give us the kind of training and preparation that enabled us to keep on producing our best.'

We can only guess, then, at what he would make of the principal sponsors who are hoping to swell their coffers by backing the Qatar World Cup. There are six semipermanent sponsors of FIFA and, at the time of writing, a further five involved with the current competition. Four of these 11 companies, three of which are solely sponsors for Qatar, produce food and drink items: Coca-Cola, Budweiser – the official beer of the World Cup (and I was, indeed, tempted to put beer in inverted commas) – McDonalds and Mengniu. The health-giving qualities of the first three products on this list are, of course, well documented; the final one may be something of an unknown.

Mengniu is a Chinese diary company, producing milk products and ice cream. In terms of its profile as the manufacturer of healthy products, it has an unpromising backstory. In 2008, it transpired that its infant formula had been contaminated with melamine, causing half a dozen deaths and 54,000 hospitalisations. The World Health Organisation called the incident 'deplorable' and at least 11 countries halted the import of all Chinese dairy products. While there were sackings galore at the top of the company and lengthy imprisonments for many involved, the Chinese state reserved the ultimate penalty for what could only have been bit-players in the dire episode. In November 2009, Zhang Yujun, a farmer, was executed for endangering public safety and Geng Jinping suffered the same fate for producing and selling toxic food.

Since then, online complaints, hastily removed by the authorities in China, have pointed out the deteriorating quality of Mengniu's UHT milk, with evidence being found of a decrease in protein content and a concurrent increase in harmful bacteria. It is unclear whether it was this that influenced the Spanish company Danone, which has successfully convinced people that glugging their stuff every day does them good, to terminate their relationship with Mengniu. They did so in May 2021. It seems reasonable to suggest that they may have made this decision before global audiences could join any dots connecting them to this profitable but tainted giant. The press release announcing the sale of their stock in the company made no comment about any health-related issues, preferring to concentrate on how the yield of €1.6bn euros would be 'returned to shareholders through a share buy-back programme'. Mmmmm.

Tasteless beer, fizzy pop, burgers and dodgy ice cream. Nigel Winterburn and his pals probably had plenty of afternoons indulging in such illicit pleasures. Speaking to the *Daily Mirror* in 2016 about Wenger's regime, he confessed, 'To be honest, it didn't have too much of an effect on me … I mean, you can dictate what players eat at the training ground, but there's nothing you can do once they leave, is there?' As the menu choices that will flash on the hoardings during the world's premier football competition, these items seem a touch incongruous. We can be pretty certain that Arsene would be shuddering at the sight of them. Maybe. Perhaps FIFA's chief of global football development has simply resigned himself to the enterprise he's thrown in his lot with – and the name of this particular game is making money, even if he'd argue that he intends to spend it wisely and for the good of global football in the future.

Whether or not he was aware of it, the man responsible for Arsenal's astonishing success during his tenure – league champions on three occasions, FA cup winners on seven, 17 successive appearances in the Champions League – could well have taken his cue from a former Arsenal stalwart. Peter Hill-Wood was chairman of the club in 1979. It was the point at which clubs and TV companies first had to confront the implications of advertisers' slogans on the front of shirts – an issue that was particularly acute when it came to those clubs appearing on BBC, where advertising of any sort was prohibited. Hill-Wood, like many of us to this day, was not enamoured of the aesthetics of the branding of traditional shirts. That was, until economics stepped in. 'I was against advertising and sponsorship more than anyone,' he explained. 'I felt we would be losing a bit of our identity, but I have been persuaded the other way.' Forty years on and, one imagines, the sainted Arsene would have been nodding ruefully along.

If most of us have learned to live with the heavy imprint of the sponsor crowding out our club badge, it's possible that change might be on the way. Legislation is churning through to prevent players from the 15 clubs in England's top two divisions currently sponsored by betting companies to remove their trademarks from players' chests. The promotion of tobacco belongs to the distant past, as does alcohol, and shirts designed for children usually bear the mark of products and organisations that are significantly more wholesome. England, in common with all international teams, will not be allowed to display the names of any of their sponsors on their shirts in Qatar. The organisation In Brief, which deals with football and the law, offers the explanation that while this is, of course, 'to protect the integrity of the competition', the principal reason is that 'FIFA also has a duty to protect the exclusivity of the official sponsors of the event'. Naturally.

Three of the remaining seven advertisers carry the hallmark of China, meaning that, along with Mengniu, four of the 11 main backers in Qatar will come from that part of the world. As well as Mengniu, two other names will not be instantly recognised when they appear on UK TV screens, although that is unlikely to cause sleepless nights in many Eastern boardrooms. The one that might strike a chord with some consumers is Hisense, a white-goods manufacturer based in Qingdao in Shandong province. In 2015 *China Daily* was able to announce that its projected revenue in the UK for that year would be in the region of £32m as it established its place in that market. In the seven years since that projection, the company's overseas reach has expanded to the point where the UK PR agency Cision reported that in 2020, notwithstanding the effects of the pandemic, its total overseas revenue was £5.82bn. That's a lot of fridges, TVs and washing machines – you know, those things that clean up dirty stuff.

Two very large versions of Hisense's tellies are on display at Elland Road, where the firm signed a two-year deal with Leeds United in 2020 to become an official partner. The smaller version of this product is reviewed with moderate enthusiasm by tech websites. Mostly made in Slovenia, the firm made nearly a third of its 6,000 employees in that country redundant in 2020. A year later, Hisense had to sheepishly reveal that an employee at its Australian organisation had fleeced it for around $2.5m over nine years, squirrelled away in nine separate bank accounts. An official statement from the company expressed disappointment that the employee had 'seriously deviated from Hisense's core values of honesty and integrity' and had 'slipped into irreversible crime for personal desires'. There might just have been some quiet smirking from sacked workers in parts of Ljubljana.

Not, of course, that a few lost jobs in a distant European reservoir of cheap labour would register in Xi Jinping's corridors of power. There's a bigger world to win in the minds of the Central Committee and, for

Xi in particular, the people's game has a part to play. In 2014 he publicly announced his 'three World Cup dreams', which were to qualify for and host the event, with the ultimate goal of 'winning a World Cup title'. Insider reports suggest that the great leader does, in fact, enjoy and understand the game, but his interest reveals a somewhat wider purpose.

Informing much of how China conducts itself on the world stage is the Belt and Road Initiative (BRI). Readers can relax: I have no intention of embarking on a convoluted explanation of the geopolitical and macro-economic implications of this major plank of Chinese political policy. For the sake of neatness and simplicity, the definition from Chatham House, the respected international-affairs think tank, provides a helpful overview. It calls BRI 'an ambitious plan to develop two new trade routes connecting China with the rest of the world' before going on to explain that this 'is about far more than infrastructure'. Its principal aim, unsurprisingly, 'is to develop an expanded, interdependent market for China', which, in its turn, will 'grow China's economic and political power and create the right conditions for China to build a high technology economy'. And take over the world – but they don't write that bit down.

Much of the activity generated by BRI is to be found in Asia and Africa, but Europe is certainly not off limits for this ambitious programme. China's clear interest in UK enterprises is there for all to see. In 2020, the Tou Ying Tracker, an annual analysis of China-UK enterprises, identified 838 Chinese businesses in the UK with an annual revenue of £5m and over – an increase from 795 in the previous year. These same companies accrued a total of £92bn in revenue in that time. Which kind of begs the question, if you'll excuse some narrow parochialism, as to why Chinese people seem incapable of running a football club. Of the three championship clubs under their stewardship, two – Reading, and yes, I know, Birmingham City – have recently suffered points deductions for breaching financial regulations and now habitually flirt with relegation to the third tier. Many supporters at West Brom have become increasingly disillusioned with owner Lai Guochuan and it is only at their sort-of neighbours at Wolves where Chinese ownership has brought anything like consistent success.

Unlikely as it may seem, this haphazard control of unglamorous football teams (oh, I can hear the squeals from Molineux and the Soho Road as I type) would not be well regarded by the apparatchiks – assuming the situation ever crossed their radar. As far as BRI is concerned, sport in general, and football in particular, is an area of genuine interest. The Sports Tourism Action Plan specifically states that Chinese entities should encourage regions to develop distinctive sports tourism models to suit local market conditions. While that might not necessarily mean refurbishing the gents at St Andrew's (not a random choice of example, by the way) the more glamorous surroundings of the Corniche at Doha must look much more promising.

That's what the two remaining Chinese sponsors, Vivo and the Dalian Wanda Group, are probably thinking, anyway. The former makes smartphones and accessories and has a huge global reach. In terms of sports sponsorship, it has some pedigree, having been a principal backer of cricket's Indian Premier League since 2015. This relationship hit a hiccup in 2020 when the Board of Cricket Control in India (BCCI) thought it inappropriate to have a Chinese sponsor while military skirmishes were taking place on the countries' borders. Such principled opposition was, however, short-lived. The BCCI, which has its own idiosyncratic take on financial probity, promptly reinstated the relationship for the following year. Principled actions will only take you so far, after all.

Dalian Wanda is the very epitome of what BRI is out to achieve. With financial interests ranging from everything to construction to entertainment to real estate and healthcare, and with various points in between, it ranks 28th in its country's top enterprises and features on the prestigious *Fortune Global 500 List*. In other words, it's a very big beast indeed. Like Vivo, it has previous in terms of sponsoring sport. It was once a major patron of the Chinese Super League as well as holding interests in Dalian Shide FC, a club that has since gone through a dazzling array of name changes before ending up as Dalian Professional FC and making mid-table mediocrity an enduring feature of its existence. It has a reach into European football, with Atletico Madrid's home ground branded as the Wanda Metropolitano. With its eyes on everything from theme parks to cinema complexes to breweries, it is a restless organisation that will see Qatar as an important showcase.

The four sponsors that remain, all of them permanent features of FIFA's portfolio, are bona fide worldwide brands: Adidas, Hyundai, Visa and Qatar Airways. Launched in 1994, the latter is an unmitigated success story in the world of air travel. Serving 150 destinations, it has looked to the high end of the market to stamp its presence. Its Qsuites feature double beds in business class as well as the facility to format the layout of seats to form private group or family areas. It offers a world-spanning menu and a mind-boggling array of entertainments on large, HD screens. And if you wish to avail yourself of these luxurious facilities on a flight from London to Doha for a week during the World Cup, you'll have to find a mere £4,780.

They are also keen sponsors of football. Close to home, current champions of the Qatar Stars League, Al Sadd, gain from their patronage, while Argentinian giants Boca Juniors are also beneficiaries. In Europe, Belgium's KAS Eupen, along with Bayern Munich, bear the company's name, and, although the glamorous sheen of a fading Barcelona is no longer associated with the airline, it is to the bejewelled stars of Paris Saint-Germain that it now looks for its association with football success.

When it comes to France's domestic league, PSG have been champions seven times out of the last nine and won the Coupe de France six times out of the last seven. Unfortunately for them, the old joke applies: what's the similarity between Paris Saint-Germain and a three-pin plug? Neither of them works in Europe. Defeated finalists in the 2020 Champions League final, this marks the pinnacle of their achievement in the continent's premier club competition. For one Qatari in particular, this must be irritating in the extreme.

Nasser Al-Khelaifi – pictured on this book's cover – is a busy boy. His interest in football is a story of our times. Before the days of repressive states, dubious billionaires and faceless conglomerates grabbing football to their fragrant bosoms, club owners and chairmen came in much duller tints. Perhaps the archetypal historical example was Bob Lord.

Lord assumed the chairmanship at Burnley in 1955 and held on to it for over a quarter of a century, presiding over successes including winning the league championship in 1960. A local boy who became a self-made man, he came out with stuff that would have made your racist uncle wince. Beyond his part in creating England's champions, his main triumph was that he was instrumental in ensuring that ... brace yourself, wait for it ... 'the Jews who run TV' were unable to broadcast games on a Saturday afternoon. Square-headed, Brylcreem-ed within an inch of his life and always immaculate in his three-piece suit, Lord was a northern butcher, steeped in his home community. And to torture the butchering analogy, one of the few things that bind his ilk to that of Nasser Al-Khelaifi is that he'd have admired a man with his finger in so many tasty pies. I'll get me coat.

Like Lord, Al-Khelaifi hails from ordinary stock. However, his route from the son of a pearl-fisherman to spending time lurching round the lower, poorly paid reaches of the ATP tennis tours is somewhat sketchily drawn. Whatever his trajectory, by the age of 40 he had become chairman of Qatar Sports Investments (QSI), a state-backed body using sovereign wealth to invest in sport at local and international level. In the same year, QSI acquired Paris Saint-Germain and he became chairman of the football club. Two years later, the sporting section of Al Jazeera's global operations were rebranded as beIN Sports, from which beIN Media Group emerged and he duly became head of that as well. No doubt impressed by this restless spirit of corporate sporting acquisitiveness, the Emir, Sheikh Tamim, with whom he is reputed to be good friends, made him minister without portfolio in 2013. On his days off he serves on UEFA's executive committee.

BeIN had already acquired the TV rights for the Qatar World Cup by February 2020 when Swiss prosecutors dropped charges of bribery relating to the rights for 2026 and 2030. It had been alleged that Al-Khelaifi was implicated in a situation whereby Jerome Valcke, then general secretary of FIFA, had enjoyed the rent-free use of a villa in Sardinia valued at £1.8m in return for using his influence to help beIN access these tournaments. The court saw nothing wrong with Al-Khelaifi's involvement and he complained that 'the three-year investigation has been characterised by constant leaks, misinformation and a seemingly relentless agenda to smear my reputation in the media'. By the time he was airing this grievance, Valcke had already joined the rogues' gallery of FIFA bigwigs languishing on the dole because of their grasping cupidity. He told the Swiss court investigating his misdemeanours in 2020 that he was running out of money. 'I have started an agriculture project in the country,' he explained, 'and I hope that the harvests will provide income in the coming months.' In the meantime, he had sold his yacht and several items of expensive jewellery. Maybe his farming will teach him something about reaping and sowing.

So, in Bob Lord-type terms of who might make a few quid here, let's have a clear recap. A bloke who is mates with the host country's leader holds a significant governmental position. He also heads up the national body which has been set up to promote sport in the country and that same body also owns one of Europe's premier football clubs. He's the chairman of that club, which is sponsored by the country's signature airline, which is also one of the World Cup's main sponsors. The same bloke is also the effective owner of the TV company, which, wholly legitimately, has broadcasting rights for much of the region for the competition. He also sits on the principal committee of European football's governing body. Without doubt, he must rank as the very model of the fit-and-proper person that the rulers of the English game demand – and the definition of which they find so elusive. There are absolutely no conflicts of interest, commercial, economic or political, when it comes to Al-Khelaifi and the Qatar World Cup, and that's because he's interested in everything.

It's not entirely clear how the various internet sources that claim to know the private wealth of an individual reach their conclusions, but a figure of around $8bn seems to represent the accepted wisdom when it comes to Al-Khelaifi. On a personal level, he might not be tossing and turning too much when it comes to worrying about turning a profit. One imagines that the sponsors, too, know what they're up to. The purveyors of beer, burgers and the various brand names to be acquired through the use of a particular credit card are all spending their money for a reason. As the dislikeable Henry Ford once told the world, 'Stopping advertising to save money is like stopping your watch to save time.' The envoys of Belt and Road will have also judged that their interventions must bear fruit in time. But what of the state of Qatar itself? Will it be plumping up its own considerable national wealth?

Hassan Al-Thawadi, secretary general of the Supreme Committee for Delivery and Legacy, is entirely confident that it will be doing so. 'We anticipate the contribution to the economy essentially would be around $20bn,' he told Bloomberg TV. Others aren't quite so sure.

Professor Andrew Zimbalist, a sports economist at Smith College in Massachusetts, told the *I* newspaper that Qatar's spending is 'an act of economic madness … a vanity play' that is unlikely 'to produce any positive economic return at all'. The notion that the World Cup will place Qatar on the tourist routes is also brought into question – a doubt that I have also heard expressed by people working in the region. Dr Paul Michael Brannagan, from Manchester Metropolitan University, acknowledged that 'this world cup is meant to bring lots and lots of fans to Qatar', but expressed the reservation that 'actually it might well be Dubai and Abu Dhabi who benefit an awful lot more in tourism terms during the tournament'. It's a view echoed by football author Simon Kuper, who identifies Qatar's tourism ambition but states bluntly that 'I don't think anyone truly believes that … it's all a waste of money'.

But it might not all be about just money anyway. *Guardian* journalist Barney Ronay articulates a different sort of ambition that is recognised by a variety of commentators. 'Perhaps,' he suggests, 'the key is to realise that Qatar is speaking to its neighbours, not to us.' It is a country that only ended a major diplomatic and economic dispute with most of the Gulf states in January 2021. High tensions have stemmed from Qatar's unwillingness to distance itself from the Iranian regime so detested by surrounding states, as well as the perception of Al Jazeera's sympathetic editorial line to Iran. There is no cosy brotherhood in play between the desert nations. For Qatar, one of the wealthiest countries on the planet, staging the World Cup is as much about status as it is about money. Another *Guardian* columnist, David Conn, the *doyen par excellence* of the politics and economics of football, cites the view of Sanam Vakil of Chatham House. She explains that Qatar's World Cup bid looks as much to the Saudis as anyone. 'I see it as a quest for relevance, to be bigger in the world, which protects the security of the state of Qatar back home,' she says. 'The World Cup signifies their ambition, to project power and the sense to their own citizens of being relevant on the world stage.'

Back in 1948, members of the organising committee of London's Olympic Games probably cracked open the light ales and the sweet sherry to celebrate the £30,000 profit they had been responsible for generating. There would have been no sponsors around, poring over spreadsheets to assess the global impact of their investment. There were no debriefs in international embassies calculating the expansion of power, soft or hard. Just a touch of quiet satisfaction at a job well done and few quid made. There's no doubt that the financial outcome would have been welcome, but it was quite likely outweighed by a strong sense of satisfaction that a show had gone on that had displayed something of Britain's character to the world. They'd have been disappointed to think that this world, which some of them had physically fought for, would turn out to be so fractious and febrile 70 years on.

Nevertheless, irrespective of the cost, a marker had been put out for all nations to notice. A statement had been made about a nation's place in the world. It looks like the great and the good of Qatar in 2022, endowed with gas, tankers, money and endless cheap labour on tap, are trying to do much the same thing. For those other multinational businesses, for whom international boundaries dissolve when confronted with their financial muscle, economic and political are the driving forces behind their appropriation of, and association with, the simple game of football.

Pint and a burger, Arsene? Can't do anyone any harm.

Chapter 13

Into the wild blue yonder ... with two footballs on the pitch

I HAVE done some good in my life. On 28 November 1992, I bestowed upon my only son the footballing memory that lives with every one of us who has experienced it. We had been to football matches before that day. My local semi-pro team has always bashed around at level six of the pyramid and had been the venue for afternoons of distracted attention while chuntering with his mates, guzzling chips and, joy of all joys, running off to collect the ball when it went over the stands into the adjoining park. But on 28 November 1992, we were going to a PROPER FOOTBALL MATCH.

Sad to report, it wasn't to see the team who, I'm delighted to say, would be the cross I would bequeath to him and that, despite having a distant birthplace, he bears with all the stoical pessimism of the native. On the day in question, family matters took us close to the marvellous City Ground in Nottingham. It was there, having ascended the internal steps of the stand, and to the tune of his favourite ditty of the day – 'Would I Lie To You?' by Charles and Eddie – that he saw it first. That unfeasible gleaming rectangle of glowing emerald, shimmering in floodlights already lit on a glowering afternoon and picked out by the scarlet seats towering around it. The first glimpse of a stadium that still, on a good day, ignites the hope and sense of possibility that football can bring.

There were 19,942 people present. I hadn't bought any tickets beforehand: I walked up and gave some cash to a person at a turnstile and in we went. Over the next few years (my son was six at the time) I'd often give some money to the person at the turnstile, and then a bit more while one of us went through it and the other underneath.

Brian Clough's Nottingham Forest had made a poor start to the season and it was plain to see that the legendary manager really was becoming a shadow of his former self. Still, Forest were far too good a side to go down. Their opponents on that day were Southampton, who would end the season comfortably above the drop zone along with Oldham and Ipswich. They were blessed with the unique talent of Matt Le Tissier, who opened the scoring in a 2-1 win for his side. Forest had a late chance to equalize, but Stuart Pearce missed a penalty in the dying minutes. Nobody made a TV advert about it and we all set off home.

I was not armed with a transistor radio and nobody had thought to invent the mobile phone, so we legged it to the car just in time to catch the *Out of the Blue* thumping its jolly beat to mark the start of *Sports Report* and the classified check. This was all possible because football matches back then finished at around 4.45pm: three o'clock kick-off, two halves of 45 minutes, ten minutes for half-time and a few extra minutes if the ref could be arsed.

The news from the radio was not good. Down in the second division at Upton Park, Birmingham had been beaten 3-1, although Villa's 2-3 defeat at home to high-flying Norwich in the Prem was welcome light relief. On the way home we sang some of the songs we'd heard, with me skating over a few things that remained improper and that I didn't want his mother to hear him repeating. At the end of the season, too-good Forest went down, of course, cut adrift long before any dramatic finales. Birmingham just about avoided the drop to the third division and, thank goodness, the Villa's Premier League title ambitions came to nothing as they nestled into a chasing pack with Norwich, Blackburn and QPR, way behind champions Man United.

On 28 November 1992, ten games in the Premier League kicked off at three o'clock in the afternoon. In among the fixtures are two that would now go straight to whatever kick-off time the TV companies dictate. At Maine Road, Manchester City (ninth at the end of the season) lost 0-1 to Tottenham (eighth) and at Highbury, Arsenal (tenth) lost by the same margin to Man United, the eventual champions. The attendances at both games were below 28,000. There were just a few more at the division's game of the day at Villa Park, but a mere 5,740 made it to Plough Lane to witness the thoroughbreds of Wimbledon and Sheffield Wednesday slalom their silky way to a 1-1 draw. Sunday's televised game saw Chelsea beat Leeds with a late Andy Townsend goal in front of just over 24,000 people. The game would have been available to the 225,000 customers who reckoned it was worth around £203 per year to subscribe to the new-fangled BSkyB service.

By 1992, football was emerging from the dark days. There had been a time when to admit that you went to games to people who now just love the footy was to mark you out as some sort of throwback or misfit. Football at top level was becoming marginally more respectable and increasingly televisual, but it still, essentially, mirrored the game it had always been. The Arsenal line-up against United featured nine Englishmen, with the only continental glamour provided by two Scandinavians – John Jensen and Anders Limpar. Their opponents all hailed from the UK apart from Irishman Denis Irwin and their own Danish import, Peter Schmeichel. Of the 22 clubs in the Premier League, one was managed by an Irishman – Joe Kinnear at Wimbledon. There were four Scots, a Welshman – Mike Walker at Norwich – and the remaining 16 were English. Of the 22, all but one, Alex Ferguson, had significant experience of playing football in England, most of them in the top division. Seven of them had played for England.

In those less precious days, football's love affair with alcohol was brazen. Liverpool, Spurs and Blackburn disported themselves with the logos of Carlsberg, Holsten and McEwans respectively. Forest had a rather more homely – and diverse – take on beery matters. Their home shirts were sponsored by local brewery Shipstones and when they went away, they bore the imprimatur of Canadian brewers Labatts. Six teams were associated with technical companies, including three that made those computer things. QPR had thrown in their lot with the Classic FM radio station and, rather endearingly, Ipswich remained true to form and looked to Fisons, manufacturers of horticultural chemicals, as their backer. There wasn't a bookie in sight.

In short, football had yet to become a marketable product or an entertainment entity. For the avoidance of doubt, this is not to suggest that the game, either domestically or internationally, was living through a golden age. Account after account from those close to the action reveal multiple episodes that expose everything from financial misdemeanours to racism to misogyny through to a complete disregard for player welfare. But for many decades, football generally remained firmly on the back pages unless the exploits of those tabloid favourites, football's overpaid nancy-boys, provided some welcome, lurid copy. And while clubs were most definitely not owned by the people for the people, neither were they in the crosshairs of intra-national adventurers of various sorts. And players definitely didn't tweet pics of their living room. Or if they'd kicked a cat.

This snapshot of the game's recent past isn't the equivalent of a dog-eared remnant in a neglected album. Much of football still connects to what's been described. Teams are still supported by people who happily arrange their lives in order to see them. Football inspires loyalty and friendship and is a force for good in the lives of many people. Local businesses and enterprises are happy to be associated with their own club. Forgive the plug, but in *Project Restart* I was able to paint a picture of how, at every level, football connected with its communities at the time of the Covid crisis to provide service and support. All of which brings us to football's central paradox as it approaches this most singular of World Cups.

The competition will play out against a shimmering backdrop of gas-and-oil megabucks, glittering stadia, smooth glad-handing and virtue-signalling about everything from social liberalism to greenwashed messages of sustainability. If previous tournaments are anything to go by, heads of state will pay flying visits should their teams reach later stages and cameras will dutifully capture their reserved – and usually bemused – reaction to events on the field of play. There'll be ceremony and, almost certainly, respectful reverence displayed to local customs and expectations. Some may remain true to their convictions, but many stars of stage, screen and recording studio will, effectively, play dumb and grant the stamp of their brand's approval on the Qatar regime. Of one thing we can be sure: a huge, corporately backed, multi-national, global TV event will take place and the great and the good from dozens of walks of life will be muscling in to make sure they get noticed. While they're doing so, footballers will be trying to win matches – it's what they do.

There is little doubt that even before it has started, this is a World Cup that has made a significant impact on world football. Its effect could go deeper yet. Looking at the documentation, it's impossible to know whether those who submitted Qatar's bid genuinely knew that, if successful, it was inevitable that the competition would not be played in July – the time when all the world's major leagues could adjust their schedules accordingly. But if concrete evidence is not available, the bidders might have looked at the practice of some of world football's major stakeholders and reckoned that rejigging local fixtures wouldn't be too much of a problem. After all, one of the world's biggest clubs had let that particular genie out of the bottle some time ago – although, to be fair, they might not have been complete masters of their own fate.

In the summer of 1999, it transpired that Manchester United, the holders of the FA Cup, would not play in the forthcoming season's trophy. FIFA had decided that it was time to stage a world club championship in Brazil in January 2000. Since 1960, the champions of South America and Europe had matched up for a single game to contest the Intercontinental Cup. It was not overseen by FIFA and, in keeping with the knock-out format of the main cup competitions on both continents, was a one-off, winner-takes-all affair. From 1980, the game was played in Japan, almost always in Tokyo but with Yokohama hosting the odd game. In November 1999, Manchester United beat Palmeiras 1-0 in the Japanese capital and were champions of the world. Once the rejoicing had subsided in Amersham and Woking, nobody really took a blind bit of notice. But FIFA had plans.

In all honesty, to claim world dominance on the back of a game played out to the delight of the Tokyo public – over 53,000 of them turned out – is a touch vainglorious. The governors of the world game probably had an argument on its side when it came to expansion. If its brief was to grow the game beyond its traditional strongholds, then a championship decided by an exhibition between two of the old guard didn't fit the bill. In among the heavyweights came South Melbourne, Raja Casablanca and Al-Nassr of Saudi Arabia. All of them invited to trudge through group games and a subsequent knockout in the early weeks of January 2000 – and cutting across one of English football's *jours de fete*, the third round of the FA Cup. And if that, in itself, presented United with a dilemma, there were yet more complications to navigate.

Pressure came from various quarters to persuade United to participate in Brazil. Not to do so, it was put to Alex Ferguson and club officials, would be to snub FIFA just at the time when England's 2006 World Cup bid was gathering steam. Tales surfaced of fraught, expletive-riven encounters between Ferguson and politicians Tony Banks and Kate Hoey, once it emerged that the manager would sooner stay at home and protect the integrity of the famous old competition. The *Daily Mail* reported that he had even attempted to consult Tony Blair – the two men were reported to greatly admire each other – only for the prime minister to give priority to a chat with Slobodan Milosevic in an attempt to get him to withdraw his troops from Kosovo. In the end, with the FA having refused the compromise of United fielding a weakened side, Ferguson's team was forced to withdraw from the cup. The only winners in the whole circus were Darlington. The gap in the third-round draw was filled by the winners of a lucky-losers ballot that earned the Quakers a bonus trip to Villa Park, where they lost 2-1.

United dutifully set off for Brazil where, by all accounts, they didn't try very hard and were soon eliminated after poor results against Mexico's Necaxa and Brazil's Vasco da Gama. 'It turned out to be a disaster for us,' Ferguson admitted some years later. 'We did it to help England's World Cup bid. That was the political situation … I regretted it because we got nothing but stick and terrible criticism for not being in the FA Cup when, really, it wasn't our fault.'

The hosting bid, almost inevitably, went nowhere; Germany, just as inevitably, held the competition a few months after Milosevic was found dead in his cell in The Hague while on trial for war crimes. And Ferguson might just have had his tongue firmly lodged in his cheek when talking of disaster. 'It was a great two-week break,' he later said of the Brazilian adventure. A refreshed United came back to romp away with the league by 18 clear points. Quite what the effect of players returning to domestic leagues in January 2023 might be, whether on the back of triumph or disappointment, will be interesting to observe.

That precedent may have taken place over 20 years ago but the very fact that it has made its mark on the history of the English game since is telling. It's difficult to think that it may not be a portent of things to come. The disruption of Qatar will set plenty of minds racing about challenging the sacrosanct nature of some established domestic competitions. Competitions which, in increasing numbers, are becoming ever less competitive – a situation ripe for those still eyeing up the prospect of franchise-dominated Super Leagues.

In April 2021, the first shot at establishing a European Super League (ESL) was made by those in charge of a dozen of Europe's top clubs. Within hours it was met with a mixture of ridicule and venom from everyone from supporters' groups to senior politicians. The proposal was taken off the table in a matter of hours as its vision of exclusivity and monopoly affronted almost everyone associated with the game. Above all, for generations nurtured on dreams of promotion and dread of relegation, it threatened to remove the vital jeopardy that is part of football's intrinsic appeal – including the 'too good to go down' trope. The notion of an American NFL model, sealed from the vagaries of fate, historical cycles and plain old payback, ran against the grain. None of which has dispelled the obstinate notion that this clumsy episode was anything but a first shot.

Days after the collapse of this first attempt at a breakaway, American sports and business analyst Simon Chadwick told CNBC that 'Europe will get a Super League by a different name' and that it was 'a case of when, not if'. He probably didn't have to exercise his professional skills too energetically to reach that conclusion. From 2024, the Champions League – that's the league of champions that includes teams who come fourth in their domestic leagues – will expand to 36 teams. Group stages of four teams will give way to a league system whereby each team will play ten games, home and away, to five others ranked according to their strengths by UEFA. The top eight will go through to a 16-team knockout and numbers nine to 24 will slug it out in a two-leg play off to reach that same stage. It could conceivably take 19 games to win the competition – half as many in the current Premier League season. Recent talk of including teams with 'traditional' levels of success has stuck its ugly head above the parapet. If it walks like a Super League and quacks like a Super League …

For those who see this land of promise as being within reach, the Champions League already holds out the possibility of life-changing sums, even at the earlier stages of the competition. Those pre-season jaunts to unfamiliar places, which, for the likes of Celtic and Rangers, can mean getting to group stages, are worth a basic yield of over £15m. When Spurs reached the final in 2019, it was estimated that their efforts produced an overall sum of £100m from one season alone. Football finance expert Kieran Maguire points out that, by coincidence, this is the total sum supplied by Jack Walker to realise his dream of making Blackburn Rovers the champions of England in 1995. Fellow expert David Goldblatt also invokes this echo from the past. Recalling those ancient times when Nottingham Forest were twice champions of Europe, he observes that 'this success didn't turn [them] into an economic powerhouse ... whereas now it catapults you into a completely different economic zone'. He goes on to explain how 'we've seen this with smaller European nations, where one club manages every year to get to the qualifying stages – not even the group stages – and that's enough to give them an unbeatable head start'.

This head start plays out in ever-diminishing levels of competition in Europe's leagues. Journalist Miguel Delaney's detailed work on this reveals that far from being more democratic and inclusive – the buzz words for which both UEFA and FIFA habitually reach – this concentration of funds and self-perpetuating cycles of success create an ever-narrower band of clubs who can ever join football's elite. He points to the increasing frequency of multi-award seasons for teams in Spain, Germany, Italy, France and England. There have been 'invincible' seasons in Italy, Portugal and Scotland and 100-point seasons in Italy, Spain and England. In 13 of Europe's 54 leagues, single teams have seen their longest runs of titles happen in the last decade. The gap between clubs in the same domestic leagues also manifests itself in the increasing number of four- or five-goal thumpings interspersed with the greater frequency of downright thrashings.

Predictability becomes the order of the day, with romance increasingly in short supply. You can be pretty sure that this observation is true when those hard heads at Deloitte's Football Money League warn of 'a situation where on-pitch results are too heavily influenced by the financial resources available' resulting in the removal of the unpredictability that should characterise competitive sport. Or when even UEFA itself notes that among elite clubs, impactful mistakes have all but disappeared from games involving top clubs. Especially against Watford. No, of course they weren't quite as bluntly specific, but it's what they meant.

There is every possibility that the Qatar World Cup cracking into the tradition and practice of the main leagues could yet help to prize open creaking floodgates holding back the flood of the Super League. And, in the form of a crowbar being quietly but determinedly applied by FIFA president Gianni Infantino, there is added pressure to break them open. He is the driving force behind the idea of a World Cup every two years. European football exper Gabriele Marcotti, although not convinced that Infantino will win the day, is reluctant to dismiss the idea entirely. Looking at 2024 – the year that the Champions League will expand – he acknowledges that a biennial competition would mean redrawing the international match calendar, 'the master document that determines when football is played' at club and international level. When that time arrives, he explains, 'the game's power brokers will have to come up with a new agreement regardless of what happens with the World Cup … but it is a delicate ecosystem, balancing the needs of clubs … with internationals.'

The selection of Qatar as host has upset football's apple cart in a whole range of ways, forcing many of us to rethink ingrained assumptions about where the game's home may be in a changing, volatile world. It could yet be the catalyst that prompts a change to those deep-seated patterns of how and where the game is played. Possibly. It all depends what we mean by 'the game'.

I am approaching my allotted three-score-and-ten. A gentle round of golf with other gentlemen of my advanced years necessitates a jolly good soak and a proper night's sleep to ward off the inevitable creaks and groans that will beset my body next day. And yet … and yet. On those crisp Sunday mornings when the shouts and calls from the local playing field carry in the winter air, a primal, unreconstructed part of my brain tells me I ought to be out there playing football, not contemplating the crossword over a nice cup of tea. That same instinct will tell me, whatever the weather, to stroll down to watch football at level six – or below – rather than slump in front of drivelling TV in the warm. I'm unconcerned about invoking the cliché – football is in my blood. And there are millions who are similarly afflicted.

Is it the blood of Nasser Al-Khelaifi? Or Gianni Infantino? I'd like to bet that they'd say it was. What's more, they'd argue that their actions will generate more devotees like me from a varied range of backgrounds and traditions. The bottom line remains that there is every chance that the Qatar World Cup will be instrumental in shifting the landscape against which top-level football will be played in the coming decades. It will remain a magnet for commercial powers looking for somewhere to showcase their wares. It will become the medium through which millions of computer games are sold and billions of dollars made from advertising everything from hair gel to heavy-duty cranes and excavators. But none of that will ever change a kid's wonder at that first glimpse of emerald turf or an old man fancifully and momentarily thinking he could pull on his boots one last time.

Other books by Jon Berry

Football
Hugging Strangers: the frequent lows and occasional highs of football fandom
Project Restart: from the Prem to the parks, how football came out of lockdown

Politics
Brutish Necessity: a Black life forgotten
Boomeranting

Education
Teachers' legal rights and responsibilities
Teachers undefeated
Putting the test in its place

Contact
www.jonberrywriter.co.uk
Twitter: @jonberry1875
https://www.facebook.com/jon.berry.7587/

About the author

Jon Berry is former schoolteacher and, more latterly, an academic who is now enjoying semi-retirement. A contented grandfather living in Hertfordshire, he doggedly shells out each year for his Birmingham City season ticket in an enduringly worrying example of hope over experience. As well as football, he writes and blogs about politics and education – and all points in between. His latest non-football book, *Brutish Necessity*, tells the forgotten story of the last man to be hanged in Birmingham in 1962 and will be available later this year.